Contents

Introduction

This publication comes at a propitious time.

In the aftermath of the financial crash, the debate about the future of the City and financial services in Britain involved more heat than light. There was a wholly understandable outburst of public anger at those who had been guilty of mismanagement in the banking sector, particularly because some of them were reaping unjustified and colossal rewards for their failure at the taxpayers' expense. Banker-bashing became the new national sport.

But if the outrage was unsurprising, and even justified, the public and political debate that followed was often ill informed and unedifying. The emergent Occupy movement never developed a coherent manifesto and essentially ended up simply amounting to a cluster of people sitting around in tents at St Paul's Cathedral, perhaps causing as much of public relations problem for the Church of England as for the bankers themselves.

Politicians of all stripes mounted the bandwagon, often with undisguised glee. A bidding war ensued about who could be toughest on the financial services industry. A myth was perpetuated that the City had been allowed to run amok in some wholly unregulated, Wild West, anarchic fashion. Whereas, in fact, as this publication shows – financial services were a highly regulated and badly regulated sector.

The essays in this volume seek to shine some genuine light onto a complex and crucial area of public policy which has often been reduced to a shouting match.

Anthony Wilkinson, Abhishek Majumdar and Duncan Flynn each provide cogent analyses of the importance of the City, in its many different facets, to both the British and global economy. Alex Deane provides an inside account of the unique and historic role played by the City of London Corporation. Tim Congdon tackles head on the assertion that financial services are "socially useless". Tim Evans suggests a radical solution – removing the state from banking and the money supply altogether.

This excellent collection of essays will leave the reader in no doubt that the City plays an absolutely crucial role in our economic life and that the problems and challenges it faces are often a result of too much state intervention and regulation, not too little.

"In Defence of the City" is an important document. Some five years on from the financial crash, perhaps the fog is finally clearing and a more reasoned, rational and informed debate about the future of our financial services sector can begin. This publication is an important contribution to that debate.

Let us hope it may even a mark a turning point at which we begin to generate greater public understanding of the vital role the City plays and how we can create the right policy framework for it to flourish in the years to come.

The Freedom Association deserves both our thanks and congratulations for bringing together this excellent report.

Mark Littlewood
Director General of the Institute of Economic Affairs

Chapter 1

On the social usefulness of Lord Turner

Prof. Tim Congdon

The allegation of 'social uselessness'

In a 2009 interview for *Prospect* magazine Lord Adair Turner alleged that much of the UK's financial services sector was 'socially useless'. Given that he was Chairman of the Financial Services Authority at the time, his remarks caused astonishment. The outburst may have been caused by a well-known feature of the UK economy, that its financial sector is large (as a share of output and employment) compared with that in other high-income European nations. In 2012 Turner published a book *Economics after the Crisis: Objectives and Means* which reiterated the central point of the 2009 interview and elaborated the argument. Despite Turner's evident dislike of the banking industry, he was in early 2013 widely tipped as a possible successor to Mervyn King as Governor of the Bank of England. *The Financial Times*, often described as Europe's leading financial newspaper, even carried a few articles championing his cause.

The purpose of this paper is to refute Turner's claim. Indeed, the paper argues that Turner overlooked a salient and well-known characteristic of the UK's financial sector, that a substantial share of its output is exported. The explanation for the UK's apparently disproportionately large financial sector is in fact largely to be sought in its global orientation and its success in foreign markets. It is bizarre,

Z/Yen Group Limited
90 Basinghall Street
London EC2V 5AY
Tel: (020) 7562-9562
Fax:(020) 7628-5751
Email: hub@zyen.com

The Z/Yen Group

In Defence of the City

A Collection of Essays

Introduction by Mark Littlewood

Produced by The Freedom Association
for the Hampden Trust

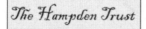

First Published 2013
Copyright © Dia Chakravarty 2013

Bretwalda Books
Unit 8, Fir Tree Close, Epsom,
Surrey KT17 3LD

info@BretwaldaBooks.com

To receive an e-catalogue of our complete
range of books send an email to
info@BretwaldaBooks.com

ISBN 978-1-909698-44-4

Bretwalda Books Ltd

to say the least, that an individual occupying a prominent position in a nation's public life could criticize activities vital to paying for that nation's imports from the rest of the world.

A zero-sum game between citizens of the same nation?

According to Turner in *Economics after the Crisis*, economies contain two kinds of activity, those which generate 'real value added', and those that are concerned with the distribution of income and wealth. Examples of the second – labelled 'distributive rent extraction' by Turner – are a bookmaker (who redistributes between gamblers) and a divorce lawyer (who redistributes between husbands and wives). The nub of Turner's critique is that finance is largely involved with redistribution rather than 'real value added'. It follows, in his words, that 'The higher the share of complex financial services in our economy, the greater the danger that highly skilled people will be attracted to activities whose social impact is simply distributive'. He fears that one possible implication is that 'a financial system could grow beyond its socially optimal size'. In other words, the basis of Turner's allegation of 'social uselessness' is that the UK has a financial sector that both takes up scarce resources and redistributes to no good purpose between the millions of citizens that constitute the British nation. This redistributive activity between the citizens of the same nation is deemed to be zero-sum and futile, and hence to have no value to society.

Plainly, the validity of the Turner critique depends on the 'output' of the financial sector being sold from one group of British citizens (those in financial jobs) to the rest of British society. This begs a vital question. Is it in fact true that the UK's financial industries – including those located in the City of London – are engaged principally in *domestic* transactions, that is, in transactions between British people and companies? Abundant data are available on the geographical split of UK financial business and, in particular, on the relative size of City's foreign and domestic revenue streams. These data demolish Turner's argument. It turns out that the City of London's receipts are dominated by *international* transactions. The UK does have financial institutions focussed on the domestic market. But their share of the nation's output, and the proportion of its resources that they use, are in line with other nations at a comparable level of economic development. The exceptional size of the UK's financial sector arises because the UK's impressive record in the export of financial services.

Turner quotes extensively from a paper by Andrew Haldane, a senior Bank of England official, in a 2010 book on *The Future of Finance*. According to Haldane, 'In 2007 financial intermediation accounted for more than 8 per cent of [the UK's] total gross value added [i.e., output], compared with 5 per cent in 1970.'

Table 1: The rising share of UK financial service exports in UK GDP

	Gross value added, at current prices, £b.	Exports of financial services, £b.	Exports of financial services, as % of GVA
1987	385.7	2.8	0.7
1988	431.2	3.0	0.7
1989	475.5	5.8	1.2
1990	518.2	6.2	1.2
1991	542.4	6.4	1.2
1992	565.8	5.6	1.0
1993	597.7	6.9	1.2
1994	633.0	8.2	1.3
1995	668.9	9.3	1.4
1996	712.7	12.1	1.7
1997	754.0	14.2	1.9
1998	794.2	11.8	1.5
1999	832.1	14.8	1.8
2000	874.7	17.0	1.9
2001	917.7	19.2	2.1
2002	963.3	19.7	2.0
2003	1024.3	22.6	2.2
2004	1081.0	25.5	2.4
2005	1139.3	29.1	2.6
2006	1204.8	35.8	3.0
2007	1274.9	47.4	3.7
2008	1312.1	54.8	4.2
2009	1280.3	48.1	3.8
2010	1327.9	45.5	3.4
2011	1360.9	48.4	3.6
2012	1383.1	46.0	3.3

Source: Office for National Statistics, with last column calculated by author

It is this 3 per cent rise – this 3 per cent supposed over-expansion – that lies behind the Turner conjecture that finance has grown beyond 'its socially optimal size'. Turner wrote a 60-page exercise for *The Future of Finance* on 'What do banks do?', while three Bank of England authors under Haldane's direction had a 40-page paper entitled 'What is the contribution of the financial sector: miracle or mirage?'. Together the two contributions took up over 100 pages and more than 30,000 words. Unfortunately, despite the abundance of words, both Turner and Haldane failed to notice that about half of the UK financial sector's output is exported! Admittedly, the exact proportion depends on definitions, but a ratio of about a half emerges from several alternative approaches. Even worse they did not notice that in recent decades the growth in the financial sector, as a share of national output, can be entirely explained by a spectacular boom in financial service exports. According to readily-available official data, the UK's exports of financial services had climbed from 0.6% of national output in 1986 to 3 ½% - 4% of national output at the end of the first decade of the 21st century. (See Table 1 above. But note that the official figures for 'financial service exports' may understate the significance of the financial sector as an exporter. Insurance is another category in the data, while closely-related accountancy and legal services are separately measured, although not functionally distinct. The point is picked up later in the discussion, where it is suggested that 'the City cluster' nowadays accounts for exports of about £85b. rather than the £45b. - £50b. given in Table 1.)

The boom in exports in this period of almost 30 years amounted to about 2 ½% - 3% of the value of GDP at its end. Rather obviously, this is the counterpart in terms of demand to the 3% rise in the share of gross value added (i.e., output) attributable to 'financial intermediation' which was noted by Haldane. How can any country be disadvantaged by having a set of industries which over an extended period of time grows its exports by 15% a year? Turner must be asked directly, 'are you claiming that – when the UK's financial services industries expanded their exports dramatically as a share of their total output – this was a sign that these industries were heavily and wastefully involved in "distributive rent extraction" between the citizens of their own country?'.

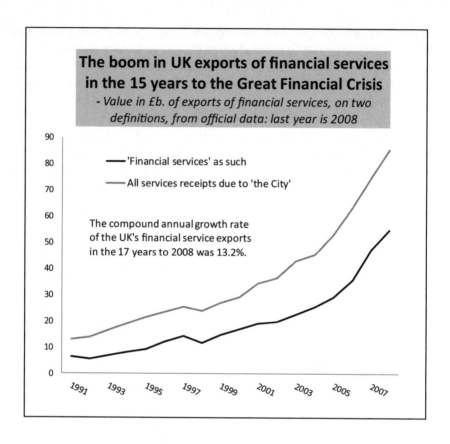

UK financial services' output as a share of world output: is it too high?

To repeat, half of the UK financial sector's output is exported, while the proportion of its output for domestic customers (i.e., the other half, about 4% - 5% of national output) is similar to that in other countries at a comparable level of economic development. Turner's claim that our financial sector is 'too big' or 'larger than is socially optimal' is therefore ludicrous if the matter is considered purely from the UK's own national interest. A quite different, and very reasonable, view is that the dynamism of the UK's financial service exports has offset the steady decline in the UK share of world manufactured exports. Indeed, the boom in the UK's financial service exports to 2008 resulted from a pattern of international specialization which was altogether desirable and sensible from the UK's own self-interested perspective.

But should we instead be thinking about the global context? Given that the growth of the UK financial sector has been made possible by its external orientation, the world marketplace as a whole might be deemed the right setting for Turner's concern about the social optimality of resource allocation. As a starting point for the discussion, we need to calculate the ratio between the UK's financial service exports and world output. Various figures can be put forward for 'financial service exports', because a range of ancillary services (in law, computer back-up and the media) benefit from 'the City cluster' (i.e., the foreign exchange dealing, underwriting of securities issuance by foreign companies, the trading of securities for overseas fund management clients, the writing of over-the-counter derivatives that enable multinationals to hedge risk, and so on, that constitute 'financial service exports' as usually understood). The official balance-of-payments figures have a split between 'insurance', 'financial' as such and 'other business' service exports. The demand for a proportion of the 'other business service' exports is – almost certainly – derived from the City cluster. While the exact proportion is open to discussion and no doubt varies over time, a reasonable assumption is that 40% of 'other business' exports can be regarded as part of the financial sector. There is little doubt that much legal, accounting and professional support work arises from specifically financial activities. If insurance and this 40% are excluded from the calculation, UK financial sector exports in 2012 were £46.0b.; if insurance and the 40% are included, UK financial sector exports last year approached £83.6b. As orders of magnitude, these numbers give us something to work on.

So we need to compare a £45b. - £85b. range with world output. According to the International Monetary Fund's latest *World Economic Outlook* (April 2013), the world's GDP in 2012 was $71,707b. at current market prices and exchange rates, and $83,140b. on a purchasing-power-parity basis. It is not clear which concept is the more appropriate as the denominator in this exercise, but – since the UK's financial service exports are of course traded – world GDP at current market prices and exchange rates may be the right one. Then the UK's financial service exports last year – roughly $70b. - $130b. at an exchange rate of $1.50 to the £ - are between 0.1% and 0.15% of world output, depending on the definitions chosen.

Table 2: The exports of 'the City cluster'

All figures below are in £m.

	A. Other business services (i.e., accountancy, law, etc.)	B. 'Financial services' as such	C. Insurance services	D. Service receipts due to 'the City' *
1991	6566	6390	4041	13057
1992	8247	5605	4826	13730
1993	8702	6885	6117	16483
1994	10198	8190	6835	19104
1995	10906	9259	7825	21446
1996	13853	12112	5739	23392
1997	14342	14175	5501	25413
1998	18662	11754	4765	23984
1999	21114	14796	3797	27039
2000	21907	16985	3421	29169
2001	25050	19173	5244	34437
2002	27178	19728	5801	36400
2003	28695	22563	8890	42931
2004	30237	25494	7755	45344
2005	32498	29141	11018	53158
2006	36668	35828	13085	63580
2007	39686	47397	11696	74967
2008	43597	54771	13242	85452
2009	44915	48114	15801	81881
2010	51148	45548	15232	81239
2011	56213	48425	15832	86742
2012	56490	45960	15078	83634

* Assumes that 40% of 'other business' arises from 'the City complex', as discussed in the text.

Source: Office for National Statistics, with column D calculated by the author.

Is the City of London larger than is 'socially optimal' relative to the world economy, given that the world is its marketplace? It is arguably quite an achievement for any nation to have a Square Mile (or at any rate an area of a few square miles) that accounts for more than 0.1% of world output, since the earth's land surface extends to about 57.5m. square miles. But how are we to say with any confidence whether the assortment of activities conducted in the City's Square Mile is 'too large' or 'socially excessive' in some sense if it does account for somewhat more than 0.1% of world output? Perhaps Lord Turner has an important new insight which enables him to say that 0.1% of world output is 'too much', too large an allocation of resources, for this particular assortment of activities. But others may be puzzled or downright sceptical. Why should we in the UK bother ourselves over misguided and wasteful 'distributive rent extraction' equal to 0.1% of world output, if that is what is really is?

And, to avoid further misunderstanding, it must be emphasized that international financial service activity is not 'distributive rent extraction' anyway. Turner is wrong to characterise finance in such derogatory terms. All that is happening is that rather bright and hard-working people in Britain's capital are being paid high incomes by international businesses for very valuable services that cannot, as yet, be obtained on better terms elsewhere. This centre of excellence depends on sophisticated information technology and telecommunications support, and in that sense is as 'high-tech' as can be imagined. The UK's wholesale financial activities may seem big relative to the UK economy, but they serve the world economy as a whole and are tiny in the global context.

Are the UK's financial services industries now losing market share?

Since the middle of 2007 UK officialdom has been engaged in a deliberate and undisguised attempt to bring the UK financial sector 'down to size'. There is little doubt that most members of the Labour government from then to 2010 were in favour of shrinking the financial sector, despite the fact that half its output is exported and that financial service exports were at the start of the crisis 20% of the UK's total receipts from exports of goods and services. Much the same statement could be made about most members of the Conservative-LibDem coalition government since 2010.

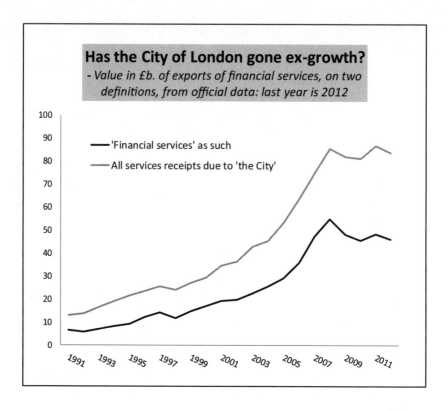

Official disapproval has discouraged new entrants from locating financial services activity in the UK, while the extra taxation and regulation have driven some business away. The peak value of the UK's exports of financial services was, ironically, in the turmoil and hubbub seen in the final quarter of 2008. Since then the value of UK financial service exports have risen in some quarters and fallen in others, but overall it has fallen from the 2008 peak. The chart above demonstrates the point clearly. (The chart presents figures on both the narrow basis, i.e., financial services 'as such', without insurance and 40% of 'other business' service exports, and on the wider basis, i.e., with insurance and 40% of 'other business'. Incidentally, it is worth mentioning that large upward revisions were made in 2011 to previous official estimates of the UK's exports of insurance. Government statisticians have difficulty tracking down new kinds of financial service activity, partly because of the pace of innovation and the volatility of different revenue streams.)

The data are open to the interpretation that the long-running boom in this part of the UK economy – a boom which began in the 1960s – is over. The City of London has gone ex-growth. This would be an unsurprising consequence of officialdom's determination in recent years to punish the UK's international financial services sector. Defenders of officialdom's approach to the City might say that the apparent stagnation of the UK's financial service exports – and the apparent stagnation therefore of the City of London – is logical in view of the major difficulties faced by all the advanced economies since the Great Financial Crisis began in 2008. However, the world as a whole – which embraces the advancing economies of China, India and so on – has grown significantly since 2008, whatever has been happening in the so-called 'advanced' nations. The value of financial services output in such jurisdictions as Hong Kong and Singapore has undoubtedly risen sharply since 2008, and they have taken market share from London as well as other financial centres in the G7 nations.

The social usefulness of Lord Turner

Has the growth of international financial services in the City of London come to a halt? As the boom in international financial services contributed about 20% of the economic growth in New Labour's first decade (i.e., the decade from 1997), it ought surely to be a matter of concern that if that growth really has stopped. The numbers set out here suggest that the boom is over and that the UK share of this type of economic activity is in decline. Perhaps the decline has not been provoked by the regulatory bank-bashing of the last few years. But the bank-bashing, plus the taxes and regulations with which it has been associated, can hardly have helped the UK to maintain – and still less to expand – the high share in international financial services that it had attained in the middle years of the first decade of the 21st century. Are the UK's financial services activities 'socially useless'? They have certainly been of huge importance to the UK in covering the growing deficit on trade in goods over the last 30 years. And what is to be said about the social usefulness of Lord Turner? Did Britain gain from having as the chairman of the FSA someone who believed that the City of London is devoted to 'distributive rent extraction' between the people and companies of the UK, even though official data show that it has been a powerhouse for generating extra export revenues?

Tim Congdon

Tim Congdon is an economist and businessman, who has for over 30 years been one of the UK's most prominent advocates of sound money and free markets. He is often regarded as the UK's leading "monetarist" economist. He was a member of the Treasury Panel of Independent Forecasters (the so-called "wise men") between 1992 and 1997, which advised the Chancellor of the Exchequer on economic policy. Lombard Street Research, one of the City of London's leading economic research consultancies, was founded by him in 1989, and he was its Managing Director from 1989 to 2001. He has been a visiting professor at the Cardiff Business School and the City University Business School (now the Cass Business School). He was awarded the CBE for services to economic debate in 1997. His latest book is Money in a Free Society, published by Encounter Books of New York in late 2011. Professor Congdon is Chairman of The Freedom Association.

Chapter 2

In Defence of a Free Market City: Time to separate banking and money from the state

Dr. Tim Evans MBA

London has the fifth largest city economy in the world, with an estimated GDP of more than $730 billion.[1] It has an economy larger than Saudi Arabia or Argentina and is a beacon for international finance, business and commerce. Alongside New York, finance has emerged to become London's largest industry since the end of the Second World War. While London is home to leading banks, brokers, exchanges, insurance companies, asset managers, private equity firms, reinsurance markets, and pension and hedge funds, at the beginning of this decade, the City handled more than 36% of global currency transactions: representing an average daily turnover of more than $1.8 trillion[2]. Today, it trades more US dollars than New York and more

---

[1]   Global Metro Monitor, Brookings Institution,
      http://www.brookings.edu/research/interactives/global-metro-monitor-3
      Retrieved 31 July 2013.

[2]   City of London Frequently Asked Questions,
      http://www.cityoflondon.gov.uk/business/economic-research-and-
      information/statistics/Pages/Research%20FAQs.aspx
      Corporation of London, Retrieved 1 August 2013.

Euros than every other European city put together.

Alongside the London Stock Exchange, Lloyd's of London and the Alternative Investment Market, more than 20% of Europe's 500 largest companies are headquartered in London. And some 75% of the Fortune 500 has key offices there.[3]

At the heart of this seemingly thrusting and dynamic capitalism is the Bank of England and the Pound Sterling. Capitalising on the English language, the UK's time zone (which enables the City to bridge the US and Asia), English contract law, a relatively benign business environment, and solid transport and quality of life infrastructure, the Pound Sterling remains the world's third most popular reserve currency, and its fourth most traded.

While today more than 500 banks have offices in the City and some 85% of the employed population of Greater London works in the service industries, since the financial crisis and downturn of 2007, the question has arisen as to the long-term impact and viability of this economic paradigm? In short, the economic crisis has raised the fundamental question: is such a system desirable and sustainable over the longer term or does it contain the socio-economic seeds of its own destruction?

Away from the popular assumption that London represents a so-called capitalist or 'free market', in reality, the current financial, banking and monetary order has very little to do with genuine market economics, free from the coerced shackles of central direction, corporatism and legislative favor. Indeed, the whole edifice of modern banking and money is built on the top-down foundations of central planning and all its propensities for producer capture and state failure.

A free and genuine market would rest on a world of private competing currencies and a banking system rooted in the laws of private property rights. Today, sadly, banking and money has very little to do with private choice or consumer sovereignty. While propagandistically appearing to be the products of a market, in reality, they are key elements in a complex web of top down statism which has placed at is heart nationalised central banks and socially divisive fiat money monopolies.

The Bank of England, the US Federal Reserve, the Pound Sterling, the Dollar, and the Euro, are not the products of free and open markets. Instead, they are politically imposed entities, borne of financial and economic Sovietisation. They exist to centrally plan, direct and control. Rooted in political power, they are

---

3   City of London Frequently Asked Questions,
      http://www.cityoflondon.gov.uk/business/economic-research-and-
      information/statistics/Pages/Research%20FAQs.aspx
      Corporation of London, Retrieved 1 August 2013.

ultimately to banking and money what British Leyland once was to motorcar production. Just as previous generations once found it difficult to conceive a world without state car production so, today, most economists and opinion formers find it difficult to envision a separation of banking and money from the state.

Far away from anything like a free market, modern economic infrastructure in the UK (as elsewhere in the world) is entirely dominated by central banking, monopolistic laws of legal tender, and deeply anti-propertarian licensing regimes for banks.

While the Bank of England is officially charged with underpinning sound money through price stability, it has overseen vast and historic debasements in currency. Since the end of World War Two, the pound sterling has lost more than 98% of its value[4]. Through the hidden tax that is inflation, the asset rich and those closest to the fractionally reserved creditism of the banks have benefited massively, while the poor and asset light have suffered disproportionate and unnecessary, cyclical, hardship.

In pricing money artificially cheap through years of low interest rates, the central planners of the US Fed and the Bank of England's Monetary Policy Committee induced oceans of debt, malinvestment and systemic crisis. As with all ventures steeped in central planning, monopoly and the imposition of a uniformity of rules, the unintended consequences are often unspeakably damaging and dangerous.

In response, while central banks have engaged in various forms of money printing (Quantitative Easing) and balance sheet expansionism to try and contain a crisis of their own making, so sates and bloated public sectors have got into levels of debt that now risk, at some point, a monetary breakdown. Addicted to QE and low interest rates there are even those who believe that un-backed fiat money and central banking regimes have now checkmated them.

In his seminal book, Paper Money Collapse: The Folly of Elastic Money and the Coming Monetary Breakdown[5], Detlev Schlichter points out that while over the last 900 years, state authorities around the world have variously introduced paper money systems, such an approach has always ended up inducing instability and eventual collapse. Always introduced by state decree and never private initiative, all paper money systems end up either collapsing in total chaos or the situation is remedied

---

[4]   Jim O'Donoghue, Louise Goulding and Grahame Allen, 'Consumer Price Inflation Since 1750', Economic Trends, Number 604, March 2004.

[5]   Detlev Schlichter, (2011) Paper Money Collapse: The Folly of Elastic Money and the Coming Monetary Breakdown, John Wiley and Sons, New Jersey.

by a preemptive and voluntary return to commodity money. Noting that since President Nixon took the US dollar off gold internationally in 1971, Schlichter points out that "for the first time in human history" the world's economy is now on a "global standard of irredeemable paper money". Contrary to the popularly held beliefs of many in public policy, the media and financial markets, a growing economy does not require an ever-expanding and inflationist supply of money. Such an approach is not inevitable, advantageous or sustainable.

Today, with many Western governments increasingly overseeing ever larger levels of public debt which in turn could herald more monetary and banking collapses, many adherents to the Austrian School of Economics see an approaching endgame:

> "Either the authorities abandon further money printing and allow the undoubtedly painful liquidation of misallocations of capital, or they print ever more money in an attempt to postpone the correction, and in the process, accumulate ever more debt. In the latter scenario, the public will ultimately lose faith in the system. Paper money systems are confidence games. When the public realizes that the printing press is increasingly used to keep states and banks solvent, this confidence will evaporate quickly. The endgame will then be sovereign default, hyperinflation and economic chaos."[6]

From this perspective, the current economic crisis is not a product of capitalism or 'market failure' because there was no market in the first place. What has failed has been a highly statist and corporatist model of economic infrastructure, institutionally rooted in central banking and monopoly fiat currencies.

It was the former Governor of the Bank of England Sir Mervyn King who publically admitted in October 2010:

> "Of all the many ways of organising banking, the worst is the one we have today."[7]

---

[6]   Detlev Schlichter, (2011) Paper Money Collapse: The Folly of Elastic Money and the Coming Monetary Breakdown, John Wiley and Sons, New Jersey.

[7]   Sir Mervyn King, 'Banking: From Bagehot to Basel, and Back Again', The Second Bagehot Lecture, Buttonwood Gathering, New York City, 25 October 2010.

As a central banker he well understands that notes and coins are irredeemable. The promise to pay the bearer on demand can only be fulfilled with another note, with the same face value, issued by the state. When this state money is deposited at a bank in exchange for a promise to return the nominal sum on demand, it becomes the bank's property and, in accounting terms, a liability. This is an important point: the money is no longer the private property of the depositor. As modern banks do not retain a full reserve on demand deposits, in reality, they are inherently risky investment vehicles subject to periodic losses of confidence and runs. When gold was money, fractional reserves on demand deposits explained how banks created credit. Today, that credit expansion process is no longer bounded by the redemption of notes, coins and bank deposits linked to gold.

Moreover, as licensed banks are funded by demand deposits and create credit on longer terms, states have been progressively suckered into providing forms of taxpayer-funded deposit insurance that subsidises commercial risk and proactively incentivises moral hazard. Depositors are no longer under pressure to scrutinise banks' affairs. Compounding these mistakes and creating further moral hazard are the statutes of limited liability. Today, they ensure no one taking commercial risks in banks stand to personally lose when things go wrong.

Again, state regulation has encouraged banks to make bad loans and dispose of them irresponsibly. Two examples are the US Community Reinvestment Act and the present UK government's politically motivated interventions to 'promote' the housing market. Having insisted banks make bad loans, the regulatory state then imposed the highly counterproductive and damaging International Financial Reporting Standards (IFRS).[8]

Combined, it is this highly statist institutional architecture and incentive structure that tripled the broad measure of the UK money supply (M4) between 1997 and 2010. For in thirteen years, one cannot increase the money supply from £700 billion to more than £2.2 trillion via credit expansion, without the ensuing boom turning to a substantial bust.[9] Eventually, the time comes when the world catches up with un-backed creditism wholly divorced from the constraining realities of tangible assets. Asset bubbles, unjust wealth inequality, the erosion of physical capital, excess consumption over savings, and malinvestment are all exposed for what they are.

---

[8]   Gordon Kerr, (2011) The law of Opposites: Illusory Profits in the Financial Sector, London, Adam Smith Institute.

[9]   Bank of England dataset LPMAUYM, 'Monthly amounts outstanding of M4: Not Seasonally Adjusted', 2 Apr 2013.

While today the City of London is a global leader in banking, money and financial services, to retain its long-term viability and success, it is vital that the current economic crisis and downturn is first diagnosed correctly and, second, that the UK overcomes massive state failure by re-connecting its economic infrastructure to genuine market principles and practices.

While this crisis first emerged in banking, opinion formers quickly transitioned to perceive it as a debt crisis. Today, the time is fast approaching when they will realise that most money is created into existence as debt by licensed banks and that, in causal terms, this is in fact a monetary crisis. It is in this context that bank reform will eventually come to be understood as a matter of monetary reform. While few authors understand this inter-linkage (see Coggan (2011)[10], Schlichter (2011)[11] and Baker (2012)[12]), future bank planning reform must also include substantive monetary reconstruction.

One of the few British politicians to understand this reality is the Conservative Member of Parliament for High Wyecombe, Steve Baker. Correctly, he has outlined the necessary goals for free market reform in the following terms:

"The privatisation of commercial risks which are now socialised.
The availability of bank accounts which provide safekeeping of money.
Choice in currency.
Prudent accounting rules.
An end to systematic intervention in credit markets by central banks."[13]

Earlier in the present Parliament, he and Douglas Carswell MP introduced private members bills to deal with four of these five issues[14]. While refraining from the full

---

[10]   Philip Coggan, (2011) Paper Promises: Money, Debt and the New World Order, London, Penguin.

[11]   Detlev Schlichter, (2011) Paper Money Collapse: The Folly of Elastic Money and the Coming Monetary Breakdown, John Wiley and Sons, New Jersey.

[12]   Steve Baker, 'Bank Reform Demands Monetary Reform' in Steve Tolly (Editor) (2013) Banking 2020: A Vision for the Future, New Economics Foundation, London.

[13]   Steve Baker, 'Bank Reform Demands Monetary Reform' in Steve Tolly (Editor) (2013) Banking 2020: A Vision for the Future, New Economics Foundation, London.

[14]   The Financial Institutions (Reform) Bill; the Financial Services (Regulation of Deposits and Lending) Bill; the Currency and Banknotes (Amendment) Bill and the Financial Services (Regulation of Derivatives) Bill.

abolition of credit market intervention by central banks, they have nevertheless mapped out a clear and practicable path to deliver a free market in money and banking.

Proposals for constitutional fiat money are in the tradition of Peel's 1844 Bank Charter Act and Irving Fisher's proposals for 100% Money. The essence of their reforms is to separate the monetary and credit functions of the banking system by requiring a 100% reserve for demand deposits. As such, bank runs become impossible, banks cannot create money and therefore a major cause of 'boom-bust' business cycles is reduced or eliminated. Current accounts become propertarian vaults for safekeeping of nominal sums and banks provide credit by intermediating between savers and borrowers.

Today, a comprehensive analysis of the benefits of market-led full-reserve banking are provided nowhere better than in Jesús Huerta de Soto's seminal work: Money, Bank Credit and Economic Cycles.[15] While some scholars might disagree as to whether fractional-reserve deposit contracts are valid or even desirable, they nevertheless foresee the:

> "...spontaneous development of a banking system comprised of a network of mutual funds, deposit institutions that maintain a 100-percent reserve ratio, and companies that specialize in providing accounting and cashier services to their customers."[16]

For Baker and Carswell, the question is how to practically and positively transition to such a system? While Huerta de Soto identifies five stages in a process of reform, including central bank independence, for Baker and Carswell, the "next and crucial step for the UK" is summarised as follows:

> "Reform is announced: bank depositors decide to what extent they wish to swap their deposits for shares in the investment funds to be created.
> "By legislative act, every bank deposit becomes the property of the depositor, redeemable in cash produced by the state.
> "Having removed the banks' liability to depositors, the equivalent assets are placed in investment funds. Shares are issued proportionately to those

---

[15] Jesús Huerta de Soto (2012) Money, Bank Credit and Economic Cycles (3rd Edition) Auburn, Alabama, Ludwig von Mises Institute.

[16] Huerta de Soto (2012) p.761.

depositors who so elected. The remaining shares are exchanged for outstanding government debt and other state liabilities, converted into bonds."[17]

Once instituted, UK banks will again be the safest in the world. Bank credit will be derived from real savings, and demand deposits will be fully-reserved under clear-cut, contractual arrangements. In the new world, savings would no longer be under taxpayer guarantee (with all their attendant moral hazard), but instead open to an emerging world of private guarantees, for competitive advantage. While investment funds would provide for those desiring short-term returns, money supply growth would now be more transparently in the hands of the central bank. It is in this setting that currency debasement to fund public expenditure would be transparently identified for what it is. In the remaining stages of Huerta de Soto's plan, he presents the practical steps to abolish the Bank of England, provide for commodity money and make real a full and free market in currency. Ultimately, he provides for complete freedom and choice in money and banking subject to a 100% reserve on demand deposits rooted in genuine private property rights and not state licensed fraud and risk.

Significantly, the Huerta de Soto plan avoids inflationism. For changing the status of demand deposits and pledging to redeem them in cash does not involve the creation of any new money. Moreover, for Baker and Carswell:

> "Expropriating those assets of the banks acquired through decades of state-sponsored credit expansion could clear the state's debts and provide for at least a substantial proportion of future liabilities to the public."[18]

Finally, the monetary and fiscal environment after the reform would herald a more honest culture in politics. As former US Federal Reserve Chairman, Alan Greenspan stated in a somewhat more lucid and illuminating previous incarnation:

> "Under a gold standard, the amount of credit that an economy can support is determined by the economy's tangible assets, since every credit instrument

---

[17]   Steve Baker, 'Bank Reform Demands Monetary Reform' in Steve Tolly (Editor) (2013) Banking 2020: A Vision for the Future, New Economics Foundation, London, pp66-67.

[18]   Steve Baker, 'Bank Reform Demands Monetary Reform' in Steve Tolly (Editor) (2013) Banking 2020: A Vision for the Future, New Economics Foundation, London, p.67.

is ultimately a claim on some tangible asset. But government bonds are not backed by tangible wealth, only by the government's promise to pay out of future tax revenues, and cannot easily be absorbed by the financial markets. A large volume of new government bonds can be sold to the public only at progressively higher interest rates. Thus, government deficit spending under a gold standard is severely limited. The abandonment of the gold standard made it possible for the welfare statists to use the banking system as a means to an unlimited expansion of credit." [19]

Ever since Nixon closed the gold window on the world's reserve currency in 1971, current monetary arrangements have not merely been tolerated but encouraged. State induced credit expansion has facilitated murderous levels of deficit spending to support state welfare over and above that afforded by the tax base. As Baker makes clear:

"This is the source of the debt crisis now engulfing mankind. A new, honest and sustainable politics would be required by the new financial environment. This proposal provides that environment and a fiscal reset." [20]

Following publication of Huerta de Soto's reforms in 1998, UK credit expansion advanced at a disastrous pace. This not only produced a range of asset bubbles but also other distortions in the structure of relative prices. Moreover, the effect on banks has been made that much worse by imprudent IFRS loan-loss provisioning and mark-to-market valuation.

An alternative route to deliver a free banking system without passing through constitutional fiat money has been highlighted in the UK by Anthony J Evans, drawing on the work of Kevin Dowd and Richard Salsman, under the title: 2 days, 2 weeks, 2 months: A proposal for sound money. It states:

"Over 2 days – ensure all operating banks are solvent:
• Deposit insurance is removed – banks will not be able to rely on government support to gain the public's confidence.

---

[19] "Gold and Economic Freedom", Alan Greenspan, reprinted in Ayn Rand, (1967) Capitalism: The Unknown Ideal, New York, Signet.

[20] Steve Baker, 'Bank Reform Demands Monetary Reform' in Steve Tolly (Editor) (2013) Banking 2020: A Vision for the Future, New Economics Foundation, London, p. 68.

- The Bank of England closes its discount window.
- Any company can freely enter the UK banking industry.
- Banks will be able to merge and consolidate as desired.
- Bankruptcy proceedings will be undertaken on all insolvent banks: suspend withdrawals to prevent a run; ensure deposits up to £50,000 are ring-fenced; write down bank's assets; perform a debt-for-equity swap on remaining deposits.
- Re-open with an exemption on capital gains tax.

Over 2 weeks – monitor the emergence of free banking:
- Permanently freeze the current monetary base.
- Allow private banks to issue their own notes.
- Mandate that banks allow depositors to opt into 100% reserve accounts free of charge.
- Mandate that banks offering fractional-reserve accounts make public key information.
- Government sells all gold reserves and allows banks to issue notes backed by gold (or any other commodity).
- Government rescinds all taxes on the use of gold as a medium of exchange.
- Repeal legal tender laws so people can choose which currencies to accept as payment.

Over 2 months – the end of central banking:
- The Bank of England ceases its open-market operations and no longer finances government debt.
- The Bank of England is privatised (it may well remain as a central clearing house)."[21]

This process quickly establishes a free banking system and the monetary incentives for honest politics. Moreover, unlike the Huerta de Soto plan, fractional-reserve demand deposits:

"…are permitted and there is therefore no provision to expropriate banks in

---

[21]   Antony J. Evans '2 days, 2 weeks, 2 months: A Proposal for Sound Money', 23 March 13, Cobden Centre, http://www.cobdencentre.org/2013/03/2-days/ Retrieved 2 August 2013.

such a manner as to offset public liabilities. However, in an environment without taxpayer-backed deposit insurance, it seems likely 100% reserve accounts would be popular. It is not clear how they would be backed by cash: perhaps banks would obtain the necessary reserves by selling assets to government in exchange for new money with a similar affect on the public finances."[22]

Today, what the City of London represents to the world is a great and shining example of the power of human creativity and initiative. Enterprising, competitive and in business to create wealth for the benefit of all, it has nevertheless be weighed down and constrained by all manner of state failures and interventionism. The unintended and dystopian consequences of its highly statist economic infrastructure is now clear for all to see.

Just as British industry was opened up to global competitive forces in the 1980s and now, gradually, the human services of education, health and social care will likewise engage ever more private provision and investment, so it is vital that the current crisis of political economy is addressed with these types of market based solution.

While the end of the old order will be marked by further bubbles, as desperate interventions are applied in an attempt to defibrillate stagnant economic arrangements, at some point it will become apparent that such interventionism is ineffectual and counterproductive. As widespread defaults and/or substantive price inflation overwhelms the state, swift action will be necessary to reinstate a genuine market in banking and money so that sustainable and legitimate prosperity can be institutionally underpinned and supported for the long term.

As in the Thatcher years, it is free-market capitalism and not more central planning that will eventually save us from the catastrophe of state interventionism in banking and money. Sooner rather than later, London will require a separation of money and banking from the state so as to ensure its sustainability and success in the twenty first century.

---

[22]   Steve Baker, 'Bank Reform Demands Monetary Reform' in Steve Tolly (Editor) (2013) Banking 2020: A Vision for the Future, New Economics Foundation, London, p.70.

Dr. Tim Evans MBA
Senior Fellow, Adam Smith Institute
Senior Fellow, The Cobden Centre

Dr. Tim Evans is a Senior Fellow with the Adam Smith Institute, Chairman of the Economic Policy Centre and a strategy consultant to some of world's largest corporations.

A former President and Director General of the Centre for the New Europe (2002-2005) in Brussels, between 1993 and 2002, he was the Executive Director of Public Affairs at the Independent Healthcare Association in London where he oversaw the political affairs and public relations of the UK's independent health and social care sector. In this role he was widely credited as being the major driving force behind the '2000 Concordat' which was described by the Financial Times as the most "historic deal in 50 years of British healthcare". Prior to that, in 1991, he was the Head of the Slovak Prime Minister's Policy Unit in Bratislava where he worked alongside Prime Minister Dr. Jan Carnogursky. In the late 1980s he was Assistant Director of the Foundation for Defence Studies. He has an M.Sc and PhD from the London School of Economics and in 2012 was awarded an MBA. In 2007, he became a member of the Mont Pelerin Society. A regular commentator on television and radio, his articles have appeared in the Financial Times, City AM, The Economist, Guardian, The Wall Street Journal Europe as well as a host of other media platforms around the world.

Chapter 3

The City of London: a unique democracy, and our greatest economic asset

Deputy Alex Deane CC

The City of London Corporation

The City of London is run by a "Corporation" – a body older than Parliament, with members elected to it by both residents and the employees of businesses in the authority's area, with votes allocated in proportion to their number of employees – a hybrid electorate system unique in the UK. The Corporation is older than legal memory, and no document exists to show when it was "incorporated" – it is therefore incorporated "by prescription", meaning that whilst it is recognised as being incorporated, its being predates any existing record to show when it happened (the protection of the rights of the City of London is referred to, for example, in Magna Carta of 1215).

Whilst a longstanding part of our national civic life, the most common reaction encountered when the Corporation comes up in conversation is mystification. This chapter is therefore simply intended to explain what it is and does, along with some statistics and information about the ongoing importance and relevance of the financial sector with which the Square Mile has come to be synonymous.

City elections

Like Parliament, the Corporation is divided into two parts – Common Councilmen (like me), of whom there are 100 (elected en bloc every 4 years), and Aldermen, of whom there are 25 (elected individually, 6 years at the most from the last election) – the Court of Aldermen is the equivalent of Parliament's upper house and the Lord Mayor is drawn from their ranks.

The City has 25 Wards. Members are allocated from those Wards to the Corporation (or "Court of Common Council") in a way akin to that in which the US Congress apportions membership of its two houses. As the US Senate is divided equally between states regardless of size, each Ward has a single Alderman; just in the House of Representatives are allocated according to the size of the population of the relevant state, the City's 100 Common Councilmen are allocated to Wards according to the size of the voting population. So the smallest wards have just two members; my Ward, Farringdon Without, is the biggest and has 10 members.

In addition to the hybrid electoral system, the City is unique in two other significant ways. First, it is not party-political – whatever their allegiance outside the Square Mile, all elected members are elected as independent candidates and no party systems or structures operate within it. Secondly, members of the Corporation are entirely unpaid – they receive no per diems, expenses, allowances or fees.

The Lord Mayor

The position of Lord Mayor of London is ancient – it has continuously been in existence from 1189. The Lord Mayor now represents the City nationally and internationally, travelling abroad with Ambassadorial status and spending months of his year in office abroad. His key responsibility in the modern age is to promote the City of London as the world's leading international finance and business centre. Working with UKTI and the FCO and TheCityUK to boost UK-based trade, the Lord Mayor in 2011/12 visited 26 countries on 13 separate overseas visits programmes.

The Lord Mayor lives in state in the Mansion House for the duration of his Mayoralty, and gives up his other work for the year of his office (and often significant time prior to it as well, in preparation for the work to come). Like all the other Members of the Corporation, he performs this duty as a public service, receiving no remuneration for the year of full time work on behalf of the City. The Lord Mayor has a charitable programme each year for which he raises (very) large funds & offers opportunities for high-profile CSR work by businesses. Mansion House facilitates around 700 events each year ranging from small business meetings to major banquets and events.

The Sheriffs

The City also has two Sheriffs (elected annually) who serve to support the Lord Mayor. The role of Sheriff is ancient and, as the name suggests, grew from responsibilities to enforce law and order but now is a civic and ceremonial function. You have to have been a Sheriff in order to be Lord Mayor.

Who cares?

I've set out all of this because it hopefully serves to illustrate the fact that the City embodies a part of our nation's history which lives on in the traditions and activities of the Square Mile to this day. The City Corporation's democratic and civic life is intertwined with, but strictly speaking separate from, the financial business done within it. The Corporation runs local government services, speaks for the City nationally and internationally, but by quirks of history which those who enjoy tradition should cherish rather than dismiss, it is produced by an unconventional route which manages organically to represent both residents and business, and to simultaneously be at (enough of an) arm's length from the day to day doings of the businesses within the Square Mile driving our national economy that it can point out shortcomings and speak truth to power to them when required.

I am a Common Councilman. To give a sense of the diversity of activity in the City, here are a few of the things just in my Ward, Farringdon Without: a ship serving as an office and events venue (HMS President – now home of The Freedom Association), a portion of the bustling Thames embankment, the Temple (home of England's barristers), a bit of Fleet Street, Chancery Lane, Smithfield Market, Travers Smith HQ, Hogan Lovells HQ, Barts Hospital, many residential properties, several churches and monuments of national significance.

Local government

The City undertakes the usual local government services for the Square Mile like any other local authority, with the obvious wrinkle thrown up by a small resident population and a whopping daytime working population. In infrastructure maintenance terms, the City is home to some of the UK's busiest stations (like London Liverpool Street on the mainline network and Bank on the tube) and the Corporation operates at a non-trivial level in spending terms on infrastructure (for example, contributing £200 million to Crossrail). Some other local tasks for which the Corporation is responsible:

- Refuse collection and disposal for some of the UK's most densely packed commercial areas: The household and commercial waste services to the Square Mile includes processing approximately 5000 tonnes of residential and street cleansing waste per annum.
- Street maintenance and lighting in some of the busiest streets in the UK: 88.8 km of streets and walkways in the Square Mile, including 7km of TfL roads.
- Planning for significant areas and iconic buildings: the Gherkin, the Heron, the Cheesegrater etc. (With special consideration given to strategic economic development). In 2012 the City considered 1,197 planning applications.
- Licensing: City workers being a thirsty lot, there are 750 licensed premises in the Square Mile! The hostelries on the avenues and alleyways of the City are packed with history and well worth exploring.
- Education: the City is home to three independent schools: City of London School, City of London School for Girls and the City of London Freemen's School. Financially sponsors three City Academies in Hackney, Islington and Southwark and continues to support them.
- Social services: the Corporation owns and manages 11 housing estates – two within the Square Mile, and the other nine across other London boroughs (2,761 properties in total).
- Responsible for the upkeep of the five Thames bridges running into the City – a fact that has led to the creation of one of the UK's most significant charities (below).

These services are consistently rated 'Excellent' in national surveys of local authorities.

National life

Reflecting the City's role in our national life, the Mayor and Corporation host setpiece speeches each year by the Prime Minister (at the Lord Mayor's Banquet) and a speech by the Chancellor ("the Mansion House speech").

- The City's foremost Committee is Policy and Resources. The Chairman of this is equivalent to the Council's Leader and he represents the 'Square Mile' and the City of London Corporation's views to Westminster, Whitehall and abroad. The Chairman has made international visits to the Europe, United States, China and India.
- The Corporation protects City interests in Westminster, Whitehall and Brussels – that is to say, it lobbies.
- In furtherance of the City's position as a financial centre the Corporation takes positions on issues which are political: for example, the Corporation has advocated expansion of Heathrow as London has an ongoing need for a functioning and successful hub airport, and lobbies for the relaxation of visa requirements for business visitors and skilled workers.

But most of all, money is what makes the City relevant and important, in two senses – the money made in business there, discussed below in the section on finance, and the money the City of London Corporation has itself:

- City Fund: a fund which meets the cost of the City of London's local authority, police authority and port health authority activities. Generates rental & interest income to help finance these activities. In common with other local authorities, receives grants from central government, a share of business rates income and the proceeds of the local council tax. Current City Funds assets: £1.06b.
- City Cash: an endowment fund built up over the last eight centuries. Income derived mainly from property, supplemented by investment earnings; used to finance activities mainly for the benefit of London as a whole but also nationwide. Management & conservation of 11,000 acres of open space, all of the Lord Mayor's activities, the markets, three of the highest achieving independent schools in the country and the Guildhall School of Music and Drama, the banquets for visiting Heads of State and dignitaries – all paid for by City's Cash at no cost to the public. Current City Cash assets: £1.319b.

- Because of its very low resident population and high daytime population, the City is (uniquely) allowed to set its own business rate – it can be higher or lower than the National Non-Domestic Rate determined by central government for the rest of the country.

Finance and the City: where the money is made

The Square Mile is the traditional home of finance in the UK. Today, 380,000 people work in the City of London (with an additional 130,000 in Canary Wharf).

- The City of London's contribution to the national income is estimated at 3.1% of the total, while financial services represent 18.4% of total national income (or gross value added) in the whole of London. The financial services sector accounts for 8.6% of the total national income of Great Britain.
- The financial services sector as a whole made a total tax contribution of £63bn in the tax year to March 2011, representing 12% of total government tax receipts. This figure includes taxes paid, as well as taxes collected, by the sector. It's well worth noting that bonuses paid to high-achieving individuals in the sector, which sometimes attract negative publicity, usually see more than half paid to the taxman).

Diplomacy

- As an ancient institution with the prestige and premises (and money!) to carry out large scale banquets, the City welcomes world leaders on behalf of the UK Government (at the City's cost, not the taxpayer's). State visits by foreign leaders usually involve two banquets – one at Buckingham Palace, one in the City (at the Guildhall or Mansion House). These cost several hundred thousand pounds a time.
- The City promotes of London as the world leader in international finance and business services, particularly through its Lord Mayor. It is a consultee on any government consultation in the field, with a voice that is listened to and respected.

Open Spaces

The City has open spaces within its boundaries but more significantly the City has accumulated responsibility for several large areas outside it as other local authorities asked the City to take them on. The City manages c. 11,000 acres (4,047 hectares) of historic and natural green space in the UK: beyond all the open spaces in the City, this includes Hampstead Heath, Burnham Beeches, Highgate Wood, Epping Forest, Queen's Park and West Ham Park.

Law, order and public health

The Corporation:

- is the City of London Police authority – the City provides the UK's specialist fraud investigators and there is a separate police force for the Square Mile.
- Provides the facilities for the Central Criminal Court at the Old Bailey & plays an ongoing in running it in both ceremonial and, more importantly, funding terms (which is seriously expensive).
- Is the port health authority for the River Thames, covering the tidal Thames from Teddington Lock to the Thames Estuary. It is therefore responsible for port health functions on the Thames, including the ports at Tilbury, Thames port, Sheerness, London City Airport and the proposed London Gateway.
- Runs the Heathrow Animal Reception Centre which in 2012 dealt with over 63,000,000 individual animals.

Arts and heritage

In addition to being home to many historic buildings (such as St Paul's and many other Wren Churches, the Mansion House, the Bank of England), the City is home to and runs The Barbican Centre, The Guildhall School of Music & Drama, The Guildhall Art Gallery, The Museum of London.

The Corporation is one of the most significant art sponsors in the UK, with an annual spend of c. £60m, the 3rd highest in the country. The City owns and maintains the Monument, which attracted 217,063 visitors in 2011/2012, and Keats House in Hampstead, where the poet John Keats lived from 1818 to 1820.

The Corporation co-funds the Museum of London with the Greater London Authority. The Museum cares for more than two million objects in its collections, holds the largest archaeological archive in Europe and attracts over 400,000 visitors per year.

The Corporation runs a number of lending libraries including the Barbican Library, Shoe Lane Library and its most recent addition, Artizan Street Library.

Markets

The City owns and operates three markets:

- Smithfield – the UK's premier market for meat. If you eat at top restaurants in London, your meat has probably come from here. It is still in the City.
- New Billingsgate – now in Canary Wharf. Britain's largest fish market, moved from the City in times when Canary Wharf was quieter – now in an unsuitable space. £200m turnover.
- New Spitalfields – moved out to Essex when the City became too busy. Europe's biggest fruit and vegetables market. £600m turnover.

Contribution to London life

- The City Bridge Trust is London's largest grant-giving charity. Dating from 1097, it is run by the Corporation and grows from the ownership of areas around the bridgeheads of bridges over the Thames. It has made £91m in grants in London since 1995. Annual donations now average £16m a year and are made in all 32 boroughs.
- Tackles social exclusion in partnership with neighbouring boroughs, provides affordable residential housing across London, with around 5,000 homes.
- New £3.28 million "Get Young People Working" initiative makes grants of up to £100,000 available to all 32 London boroughs to help 1,000 young people across the capital into employment or apprenticeships. Relevant for any apprenticeships / skills discussions.

- The London Drug and Alcohol Policy Forum (LDAPF) is the only independent body working to support policy and practice across the broad drugs, alcohol and community safety agenda. London-wide, it is funded by the City of London Corporation.
- The City has supported over 800 SMEs in the City and neighbouring boroughs.
- The City has a new £20m Social Investment Fund which will seek social as well as financial returns. It aims to use 60% of its funds to support beneficiaries in London, with 30% to support organisations which are benefiting citizens across the UK. The remaining 10% will be allocated to international initiatives. The fund was launched in September 2012, and has so far made one investment, into Oxfam's Small Enterprise Impact Investment Fund (SEIIF).

Conclusion

This overview is brief (it has not, for example, even touched on the role of the Livery companies, connected to but distinct from the Corporation itself, themselves amongst the most generous and consistent supporters of charitable organisations in the country). But hopefully it sets out the main points to be considered in defence of the civic and democratic City and Corporation. To some, these are obscure corners of our country – but they are filled with people of goodwill and decency who give up much time without remuneration for the betterment of others. As for the financial City, for all the sneering done at its expense it pays much of cost of the bills our country is racking up – whilst biting the hand that writes out the cheque may provide childish pleasure, mature reflection suggests that it's not sensible, even if you dislike the mannerisms or appearance of those doing it.

Deputy Alex Deane CC

A former Chief of Staff to British Prime Minister David Cameron, Alex Deane now provides counsel and advice to a range of companies and organisations as Head of Public Affairs at Weber Shandwick, the world's leading Public Relations firm, counselling businesses and organisations on political affairs and training high-profile individuals and companies to appear before Parliament on a range of issues. An active member of the Conservative Party since 1995, Alex read English Literature at Cambridge University and took a Masters degree in International Relations as a Rotary Scholar at Griffith University. He is a World Universities Debating Champion. A non-practising barrister, Alex is the author, co-author or editor of several books and pamphlets about law and politics. He is an elected Common Councilman in the City of London, and serves on the main decision-making body, the Policy and Resources Committee.

Alex is on Twitter at @ajcdeane.

Chapter 4

The importance of the City Legal sector to the UK economy

Duncan Flynn

The legal profession has never enjoyed an especially positive reputation in the minds of the British public. Indeed as far back as Shakespeare's "Henry VI, Part 2", Dick the Butcher was imploring the rebels challenging the English throne to start by "killing all the lawyers". Literary attitudes to the legal profession had barely improved by the Victorian era with Charles Dickens' "Bleak House" satirising the perceived futility of the legal system through the protracted fictional case of Jarndyce v. Jarndyce.

Mercifully, lawyers are now seen by most people as slightly more beneficial for the nation's wellbeing but the relationship between politicians and the legal profession remains a complex one. Whereas there is no shortage of prominent barristers sitting for all three main parties in the House of Commons, there are certainly far fewer solicitors with experience of corporate and commercial law presently lining the green benches. On the Conservative side, eminent former City solicitors include Exchequer Secretary David Gauke (formerly of blue chip City firm Macfarlanes) and former Justice Minister Jonathan Djanogly (a former Corporate Finance Partner at SJ Berwin) however they are easily outnumbered by barristers who currently hold the Attorney General and Solicitor General positions. On the Labour benches experience of City law firms appears less common with only Shadow Business Secretary Chuka Umunna (who practised as an employment specialist at Herbert Smith) standing out in the Shadow Cabinet.

There are perfectly solid reasons why this disconnect between UK politicians and City law firms has grown in recent years, most notably the significant demands placed of junior City solicitors which in some cases have seen flickering political interests extinguished at their infancy. Furthermore, as salaries at City law firms have risen, rightly or wrongly Parliamentary salaries have not kept pace, meaning for many legal professionals it is simply no longer a financially attractive proposition to make the transition from law to politics.

The days when City law firms possessed an unofficial political identity are also long gone. In the not too dim and distant past, firms such as Trowers & Hamlins and Taylor Joynson Garrett (now Taylor Wessing) were closely identified with the Conservative Party whereas left leaning firms such as Mishcon de Reya and Lewis Silkin were politically close to Labour. City law firms still work closely with senior politicians from the three main parties but tribal loyalties are much less apparent and co-operation is less overt.

Should this trend continue over the coming decades there is a danger that the gap between City law firms and the Westminster village could expand. What this chapter will attempt to do is to remind politicians of all shades why the City legal sector matters, why it is important to the UK economy and how the potential actions of politicians can adversely impact on it.

The rise of the City law firm

Many of the largest City law firms headquartered in the UK today have their origins as far back as the 18th and 19th centuries. Of the magic circle firms, Clifford Chance (the largest UK headquarted firm measured by revenue in 2010) can trace its origins back to 1802, Freshfields 1743, Linklaters 1838 and Slaughter & May 1889. These are firms which grew on the back of British imperialism with London the economic centre of the World and the growth of mercantile trade. Indeed many of these firms were founded by representatives of the mercantile classes such as the legacy firm for Clifford Chance which was founded by a fishmonger's son.

There are also other historic factors in why London was able to emerge as a legal powerhouse. The English Common Law evolved from the 12th century and established the principles of legal precedent and higher courts binding lower courts.

This relative continuity contrasted with the legal systems in other fledgling European nations which were subject to greater political instability. Moreover, the four Inns of Court which date back to the medieval times provided a high quality training ground for barristers.

However, it was not until the late 19th century that London consolidated its position as the global leader of the legal world. In 1875, the complex and chaotic appeal system which was heard through 12 separate courts was ended through the creation of the new unified Court of Appeal. In 1882, the Royal Courts of Justice were opened by Queen Victoria as a working monument to the burgeoning legal community in London. Outside of the capital, other significant changes were afoot such as the establishment of a degree in English law at the University of Oxford in the 1870s.

Over time, firms started to expand and specialise in certain spheres. Many of the now large City firms went through a number of mergers and changes in identities in the 20th century. Until the 1980s, most firms consolidated and gradually increased their workforce and revenues. The election of the free market Thatcher Government in 1979 provided an opportunity to change the face of City law firms for good. Section 717 of the Companies Act 1985 contained an express carve out for law firms which meant they were not covered by rules which stipulated that limited partnerships should be limited to a mere 20 partners. This permitted City law firms to expand on an unprecedented scale. Within a few years some of the leading City firms had acquired scores of new partners and a healthy smattering of overseas offices. In 1987, one of the most significant legal mergers of modern times occurred with the merger of Clifford Turner and Coward Chance creating the new behemoth Clifford Chance. Moreover, the changing political and economic climate in the 1980s and 1990s assisted the growth of the City law firm. Privatisation of previously nationalised utilities provided a rich seem of work for several City firms. Indeed, Slaughter & May still cite the work undertaken in "an extensive number of privatisations, including British Airways, British Gas and British Steel" as one of the "key milestones" in the firm's history.

The 1980s and 1990s saw the development of a tight hierarchy of City law firms. The so-called "Magic Circle" of Clifford Chance, Allen & Overy, Freshfields, Linklaters and Slaughter & May became established in legal parlance. A more fluid "Silver Circle" of major City firms striving for the top including Herbert Smith, Ashurst, Berwin Leighton Paisner, SJ Berwin, Macfarlanes and Travers Smith was first identified by "The Lawyer" magazine in 2005. In addition, other long established City firms have decided to narrow their focus to specialise on highly lucrative niche areas of the law such as entertainment and media, pensions or sports law. Such firms are now often regarded as "boutique" firms. Some full service provider City firms have also sought to seize on new potential growth areas such as Islamic Finance which demonstrates the truly global nature of the UK's City legal market.

Another important development was the passing of the Limited Liability Partnership Act 2000 which established Limited Liability Partnerships (LLPs). By the end of the decade, many of the leading City law firms had converted to LLPs, largely because of the perceived beneficial tax treatment for Partners under an LLP structure. This is an issue I will return to later in the chapter.

By the 2000s, not only was London the home to an ever expanding City legal market among firms headquartered in the UK but it was also the home to scores of top US firms. Some of the leading US firms such as Baker McKenzie (the second ranking US firm by revenue in 2013), which opened their London office in 1961 are long established in the UK, whereas other US firms are new entrants into the UK market. Most of these US firms focussed their practices on Mergers & Acquisitions, Corporate Finance and Banking work, reflecting the perceived rude of health of the British economy in these sectors. London is now the home to the offices of over 200 overseas headquartered law firms which merely underlines the strength of the City legal market and the importance of London as a global legal centre.

The growth of the City legal market had been dramatic in the early part of the 21st Century. City law firms were increasing their number of Partners and Associates and many City firms were entering into alliances or full-scale mergers with European or US competitors. Ostensibly, things had never seemed better but City law firms were about to be impacted by the one of the deepest economic downturns we have ever witnessed.

The changing market post economic downturn

The global economic downturn, which is widely viewed to have started in the UK in late 2007 with the collapse of Northern Rock, has had a significant impact on the City legal market. The vast majority of City firms have made redundancies, including fee earners and many have made Partners redundant. However, the brunt of the redundancies has been centred on support staff, in particular secretarial, paralegal and back office staff. Several firms have sought to reduce costs by outsourcing their paralegal functions to more cost-effective markets such as India or South Africa. This appears to be a trend which can only be expected to continue much to the concern of legal support staff for whom the outlook looks somewhat gloomy. The

Legal Education and Training Review (LETR), which is a joint project of the Solicitors Regulation Authority, the Bar Standards Board and ILEX Professional Standards, has estimated a decrease of 12.3 per cent in non-solicitor legal staff between 2011-2020 with the predicted decrease being even more pronounced among legal secretaries at 20.6 per cent.

In contrast, the outlook for solicitors is much more positive. The LETR reported a project increase in the number of solicitors between 2011-2020 of 26 per cent. For the hundreds of fee earners whose legal careers have ended abruptly due to economic downturn this is scant consolation. However, it does demonstrate the considerable resilience of the UK legal market.

However, over the past few years the economic downturn has made an impact on the revenues of the legal services market. The worst years were 2008 and 2009 which saw a reduction in total revenues of 2 per cent and 0.7 per cent based on the previous years. However, by 2010 the market was starting to recover with a 3.1 per cent increase in 2010 and a 5 per cent increase in 2011 which took the overall total revenues generated by the UK legal services market to £26.8 billion. There were similar increases in real turnover in the UK legal services market in 2010 and 2011 and while real turnover is expected to slow down in 2012, the long term outlook according to the Law Society is rosy. The Law Society estimates that real turnover in the UK legal services market is expected to increase by 4.2 per cent year on year on average between 2016-2020 and by 4.4 per cent per year between 2021-2025.

This recovery is largely as a consequence of the resilience of City law firms. In 2011, the top 200 UK law firms (most of which are headquartered in the City of London) generated 62 per cent of total turnover of the England and Wales legal industry despite making up a mere 2.1 per cent of all law firms. In 2011, the top 200 UK law firms employed a total of 37,616 solicitors which amounted to 43 per cent of the total number of solicitors in private practice.

The Magic Circle firms have been proven to be especially durable. These five firms now account for nearly 20 per cent of the total turnover generated by the top 200 firms in England and Wales. Between them they had in 2011 a combined turnover of £5 billion and four of the five firms featured in the American Lawyer's top 10 global firms by revenue. By 2011, Clifford Chance had 34 offices in 24 countries, Linklaters 27 offices in 19 countries, Freshfields 27 offices in 15 countries and Allen & Overy 40 offices in 28 countries. By any standard, these firms all of which are headquartered in the UK are phenomenal success stories which have continued to each generate revenues in excess of £1billion at the height of the economic downturn.

In order to keep up with the Magic Circle, there have been a number of high profile mergers of City firms over the past two years. These included the merger of Clyde & Co with Barlow Lyde & Gilbert, Pinsent Masons with McGrigors and Wedlake Bell with Cumberland Ellis. Overall, the evidence suggests that firm mergers or corporate restructuring have ensured the majority of City firms have emerged through the economic downturn relatively unscathed. By 2011, 62 per cent of the top 200 firms reported an increase in turnover relative to 2008 with only 15 per cent reporting a reduction. However, the economic downturn has claimed some victims in the global legal market, most notably former New York giant Dewey & LeBoeuf (which had a London office) which entered administration and filed for bankruptcy in May 2012 following severe financial indebtedness and a mass exodus of Partners. The UK market has not seen such a high profile casualty, although former top 50 firm Cobbetts (a firm with a history of 175 years) entered administration in February 2013 and was eventually acquired by DWF with resulting redundancies.

Despite the severe problems experienced by the London-based banking and finance centres, over one quarter of all English and Welsh law firms are headquartered in London with nearly 10 per cent headquartered within the Square mile of the City. Firms headquartered in the City amount to over 45 per cent of the top 200 law firms in the UK. Despite the continued hegemony of the City, there potential clouds on the horizon which politicians will need to be aware of in the coming years in order to ensure the City remains a highly competitive place to do business in the legal market.

The City is doubtlessly aided by the fact that English law continues to be the choice of governing law for many companies involved in arbitration proceedings. The 2010 International Arbitration Survey found that 40 per cent of the 136 companies responding to the survey indicated a preference for English law with the next highest New York state law (17 per cent). Furthermore, the same survey found that 30 per cent of respondents judged London to be their preferred seat of arbitration which was followed by the jurisdiction of Geneva on 9 per cent. The survey found that the location of specialist arbitration lawyers was the most important aspect influencing the choice of seat.

The global success of London's legal market is today felt in all corners of the world with the English Common Law system governing 30 per cent of the world's population and providing the basis for 27 per cent of the 320 legal jurisdictions throughout the globe. Closer to home, the UK legal market accounts for 20.3 per cent of the total European market in legal services according to Datamonitor in 2011.

However, there are some signs that this often unheralded success story at the heart of London's economy faces some serious challenges. London faces increasingly intense competition as a centre for dispute resolution from among others New York, Paris, Geneva, Dubai, Singapore and Hong Kong. In 2012, Singapore ominously overtook London as the main centre for dispute resolution for disputes originating in India. This is a sign that parties may increasingly be looking beyond the traditional seats of arbitration.

There is also a widespread belief that England's notoriously complex and sometimes tortuous planning system along with the reluctance of banks to lend to developers has adversely impacted on the Commercial Property sector with transactions of this nature involving lawyers falling almost 30 per cent from 2006-2007 to 2011-12.

A recent report by the independent membership body, The CityUK, found the while City-based firms benefit due to the success of the wider financial services industry in London, issues relating to an uncertain regulatory outlook and concerns over taxation rates, have the potential to threaten the sustained success of the City legal market. It is therefore vital that politicians who have the power to influence regulation and set the rates of taxation are conscious of the potential pitfalls of adding to financial services regulation or tinkering with the taxation regime.

Creating the right regulatory and fiscal framework for City law firms

Like so many other aspects of the British economy, some of the main regulatory threats to the UK legal market emanate from Brussels.

One such example is the potential financial transactions tax (or Tobin tax) which has the support of 11 EU Member States but mercifully not the current British Government. Seeking to add an additional levy to financial transactions seems likely to reduce the volume of deals which are fundamental to the work of many City law firms. Such a tax while pleasing the anti-capitalist far Left would pose a significant risk of choking off the recovery of the UK legal market. It is a measure which would cost jobs in the legal sector and should be resisted at all costs.

Another European Directive which has the potential to impact on City law firms in the future is the much-criticised Working Time Directive. At present, many City firms require their new fee earners (whether Trainees, Associates or Partners) to waive their rights on the number of hours they work to ensure they are not caught by this intrusive and inflexible legislation. As anyone who has worked at a City law firm will no doubt attest to, the hours can on occasions be extremely demanding. This is largely due to the fact that the City legal market is a world leader and it is not uncommon for solicitors in London to be advising clients in the Far East or the USA. While it is not unknown for junior solicitors at City firms to embellish the number of hours spent in the office in order to demonstrate their hardiness to their colleagues, there is no doubt that expectations are demanding and the occasional "all nighter" is a rite of passage for most trainees at a City firm. In return, the monetary rewards for recent graduates are very substantial and this is a trade-off that has to be occasionally embraced. While welfare of employees must at all times be paramount, an overly zealous implementation of the Working Time Directive by any future UK Government would be highly damaging for the UK legal market and would seriously risk the UK's competiveness.

Another more general factor which has done nothing to assist the City legal market is the the Eurozone crisis. Many City law firms act for clients, particularly in the field of commercial property, who have been severely impacted by the Eurozone crisis and consequently liquidity has dried up and transactions have withered away. It will be no surprise to readers of any Freedom Association publication that I do not recommend that the UK joins the Eurozone but its collapse continues to have a detrimental impact on the UK legal market.

Closer to home, the UK Government announced plans in the 2013 Budget to consult on measures which could force LLPs to pay national insurance for Partners who are currently classed as self-employed but are technically employees. As many City law firms have converted to LLPs in recent years such a reform of the LLP taxation regime would impact on many City firms. By seeking to restrict the freedom for partnerships to allocate profits among partners as they see fit, profits are likely to be lowered and it seems plausible that yet more secretarial and administrative staff could ultimately lose out.

More generally, it is apparent to me that more should be done by politicians to embrace the success of City law firms. Too often questions in Parliament from MPs on the subject of City law firms address selection criteria of candidates or pro bono initiatives but there is not sufficient focus given to celebrating the success of such firms and questioning how politicians can create an environment under which firms can expand even more successfully. Perhaps one of the reasons for this lies in the dominance of the City itself. While former Freshfields solicitor Mark Field MP (Conservative, Cities of London & Westminster) does an admirable job of championing the City legal sector (and other sectors of the City), it would be good to see some other politicians acknowledging this great British success story more frequently. However, if there is a lack of constituency interest that perhaps explains the issue remains uncovered by so many Parliamentarians.

Conclusion

For centuries the City of London has been the global leader in the legal market. It was aided by a combination of firm historic foundations, the Common law system and Britain's dominance of global trade in the 19th and early 20th century. As Britain's dominance faded, the London legal market adapted by embracing free markets and capitalising on more flexible partnership rules. Today, four of the ten most profitable global law firms are headquartered in the City of London. However, this is not something that is frequently referenced by UK politicians. Perhaps the reason for this lies in the increasing disconnect between politics and the law which I referred in the first part of this article. Perhaps it can be explained by the public's continued polite scepticism towards the legal profession which in the eyes of many people is embodied by the actors posing as sharp-suited legal eagles in adverts for companies such as "Injury Lawyers 4 u" which are routinely screened on daytime TV.

Regardless, it is time for UK politicians to focus more intently on the economic contribution the UK legal market (and in particular the City of London) makes to the UK economy.

There is also a social contribution which is frequently overlooked. In my experience of working at two top 20 UK law firms (both of which were headquartered in the City of London) I met many interesting people. Both firms employed people of all classes, of all races, of all religions and of all nationalities. They paid well and staff tended to stay for many years whether they were occupying the boardroom or the print room. I distinctly recall one octogenarian gentleman who worked for one of the firms as a proof-reader. He did not probably need to keep on working but he did so because he enjoyed working with the people at the firm. The firm was neither a sweat shop nor was it the labyrinthine dystopia frequently depicted in John Grisham novels, it was a community. Yes, everyone worked hard but they largely enjoyed their work, they got excellent results for their clients and they enjoyed the fruits of their labour, whether they were the Partner, the Associate, the Trainee or the Secretary. It has to be hoped that UK politicians acknowledge the strength of City of London legal market and resist any temptations to impose burdensome regulations or damaging taxation increases or reforms. The City of London legal market is an outstanding success story – it should be allowed and encouraged to remain that way.

Duncan Flynn

Duncan Flynn worked as a Banking and Finance Solicitor at a top 20 UK law firm. He trained at a leading European law firm based in the City of London. He now works as a Public Affairs consultant based on Chancery Lane at the heart of the UK's legal sector.

Chapter 5

Britain needs a healthy City and Fund Management industry

Anthony Wilkinson

Summary

Britain needs a healthy City and fund management industry. British financial services play a big part in the economy, generating 9% of economic output and 12% of tax receipts from only 3.5% of the workforce. That is a good ratio. Against the odds Britain remains a global financial services force. It is global number one in foreign exchange trading, international banking, Eurobonds, and financial derivatives. It has the largest asset management and insurance industries in Europe, not to mention a powerful presence in accountancy and law. Asset management provides the vital link between investors seeking appropriate savings vehicles and the financing needs of the real economy. The fund management industry's £12 billion annual revenue is more than half the £20 billion revenue generated by aerospace, Britain's second biggest manufacturing activity.

We live in an increasingly borderless world driven by the Internet, where the free flow of information (Google), good and services (DIY import via Amazon), and people (cheap travel via Ryanair) combine to break down business barriers. So sensible and competitive regulation is critical in financial services where the key asset (the staff) leaves the building every night. UK-based fund management is facing a tsunami of regulation, most of it at the European level. Increasingly intrusive regulation suggests that the EU believes that they can regulate away risk whereas in fact the opposite often occurs. The best way to reduce risk is having the right culture and putting the customer first but in many cases the opposite is happening. Fund managers (including hedge funds) did not cause the global financial crisis. The growing impression is a regulatory tilt towards continental European methods with seemingly scant regard for British interests. Britain has the largest market share in fund management in Europe, equal to France and Germany combined, but you would not necessarily think so.

Meantime, the Asian threat to the City is real. Whilst London will retain its advantages of language and time zone, Britain risks waking up in ten years time to find that London is no longer a top three finance centre. Paris and Frankfurt seem less of a threat than Singapore, Hong Kong, Dubai, or even Shanghai as China opens up its capital account. The global economic centre of gravity continues to swing East. Consumer spending in emerging countries already accounts for 15% of world GDP. In contrast the Eurozone is likely to continue to decline on a relative basis in part driven by demographics. In general Britain needs to turn away from the burden of further EU regulation and legislation and offset a growing EU trade gap through more trade with friendly Commonwealth nations such as Singapore, Malaysia, Australia, Canada, South Africa and India. UK fund management must grasp the enormous opportunity inherent in high Asian savings rates. The Prime Minister is right to focus on global competitiveness – after 14 years in Asia it feels very much to the author that the British political class has been asleep at the wheel.

Britain needs a healthy City and fund management industry

Asset management is a vital source of economic growth. It provides a link between investors seeking appropriate savings vehicles and the financing needs of the real economy.

Fund management fulfils the following essential functions:

- The channeling of capital from where it is in abundance to where it is needed. This fuels the real economy and takes the form of either debt capital (providing credit to companies or the government) or equity capital (investing via IPOs, the

secondary market, private equity).
- Sound analysis and monitoring by fund managers helps stimulate economic development through the allocation of capital to the most promising investment prospects.
- Massive liquidity provision in the capital markets.
- The British population benefit from access to a wide range of products serving a large number of markets, themes and industries. This encourages portfolio diversification and risk reduction.
- Fund managers act as "stewards" of their clients' interests.

London and Britain are still, despite the best efforts of some, a global force in financial services. British financial services play a big part in the economy, generating 9% of economic output from only 3.5% of the workforce. That is a good ratio. Of the one million people employed in financial services, only about a quarter are in London, with the remainder scattered in other locations such as Leeds, Edinburgh and Birmingham. London, which has the largest city GDP in Europe, is a global financial services force. It is global number one in foreign exchange trading, international banking, Eurobonds, and financial derivatives, and it has the largest asset management and insurance industries in Europe, not to mention a powerful presence in accountancy and law.

The table below illustrates some key statistics from the 2011-2012 Asset Management in the UK survey by the Investment Management Association:

Country Market Share in Total Assets under Management, 2010
Source: European Fund and Asset Management Association, "Asset Management in Europe", May 2012

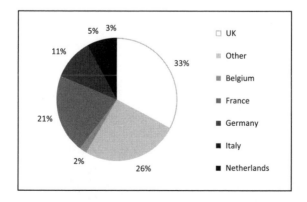

Total assets managed **in the UK** (IMA estimate), Dec 2011	£4.9 trillion
Total assets managed **in the UK** by IMA member firms, Dec 2011	£4.2 trillion
– of which managed on behalf of overseas clients	£1.6 trillion
– of which managed by hedge funds*	£185 billion
– of which managed in Scotland (12% of UK)	£500 billion
Revenue earned by **UK-based** asset management firms, 2011	£12 billion

Note*: total for UK as estimated by HedgeFund Intelligence.

Comparing the £12 billion annual revenue with other industries is illustrative – it is more than half the £20 billion revenue generated by Britain's second biggest manufacturing activity – aerospace. Moreover, £12 billion of revenue on a £4.2 trillion base of assets implies fees of 0.29% a year – that sounds like good value.

Too much of the wrong type of regulation?

In the past, the UK fund management industry was mainly regulated on a national basis. Following the dramas of 2008 and the ensuing recession, a tsunami of regulation has descended on the financial services sector, including fund management. UK-based fund managers are having to cope with a bewildering array of regulation, including:

- Revisions to European UCITS rules (Undertakings of Collective Investments in Transferable Securities) which is morphing from UCITS IV, the overhaul of the distribution of retail funds, to UCITS V (investor protection) and UCITS VI.
- Review of the EU Markets in Financial Instruments Directive (MiFID), being updated and expanded in MiFID II and MiFIR.
- Implementation of the US Dodd-Frank Act – the biggest overhaul of US financial market regulations since the Great Depression with significant implication for non-US market participants.
- The EU Packaged Retail Investment Products Directive (PRIPs).
- The EU Alternative Investment Fund Managers Directive (AIFMD, which brings traditionally unregulated or lightly regulated hedge funds, private equity funds and real estate funds under pan-European regulation.
- The US Foreign Account Tax Compliance Act (FACTA).
- The European Market Infrastructure Regulation (EMIR).

This list is by no means exhaustive and excludes Green Papers, codes of practice, and recommendations from national or supra-national committees. UK-based fund managers are now heavily regulated by European regulation and legislation emanating from European institutions like the European Commission and the European Securities and Markets Authority (ESMA). On top of this, both American and European regulatory responses to the GFC contain extra-territorial reach which makes it a lot more complicated and more expensive to operate on a global basis. In Britain, fund managers will also have to cope with the new Prudential Regulatory Authority and Financial Conduct Authority, successors to the Financial Services Authority.

It seems that asset management arms of European or EU-located banks will also be impacted by yet another piece of regulation - the EU's Capital Requirements Directive. Asset management arms of banks tend to command a higher market valuation than other trading or banking elements within universal banks' total market capitalisations. Higher asset management fixed costs imply lower margins and more cyclical risk, and therefore lower asset management valuations. This is negative for overall bank valuations – clearly unhelpful for the European banking industry which is under such pressure anyway.

In principle, many British (and international) fund management companies welcome this as a means of entrenching the single market with past European UCITS directives seen as benefiting both investors and fund management companies alike. In practice however, the mood appears to be changing. A growing number of fund managers are worried about the sheer scale of regulation which is taking up a huge amount of management time, costing a fortune in legal and compliance assessment, and potentially impacting investment returns.

Of concern too is the impression of a growing politicization of regulation, the lack of adequate analysis of the impacts of competing regulation even just within the European Union, and a leaning towards continental European business models with seemingly scant regard for British interests. In early July 2013, there was a very close vote in the European Parliament on proposals to ban fund managers from getting a bonus greater than their annual salary. This would have gone beyond planned EU limits on banker pay that will allow bonuses at twice fixed pay. Left-leaning politicians and journalists see this as necessary for consumer protection but in fact it would have been hugely damaging for the European asset management industry as there would have been a bidding war for the best trading and portfolio management talent which would have greatly raised fixed costs, thereby actually raising costs for the end-consumer and doing nothing for consumer choice. Higher fixed costs increase, not reduce, systemic vulnerability when the inevitable market downturn arrives.

In addition, higher costs raise barriers to entry and discourage new entrants. That is bad news for consumers of financial products (which is just about everybody) who would benefit much more if there were more asset management companies to choose from, not fewer. Regulators should be busy enabling a culture of transparency, where the ability of fund management professionals and their support staff to generate wealth is as directly linked as possible to the investment returns generated for the customer. The more over-eager politicians and regulators rush to regulate, the higher the cost of doing business and the lower the level of competition for the people that really matter – the customers. It is unsurprising to note that the last time a global asset management company was established in Britain was in 2007.

The bigger picture is that asset management is a global industry in a fast-globalising world. Globalisation, a process that is constantly reinforced by technological development, is irreversible (unless you live in North Korea), and is accelerating. Globalisation increases economic integration. Investors can now invest pretty much anywhere, and will gravitate to where they can secure the best risk-adjusted return. The UK's Investment Management Association surveys show a clear trend in the internationalization of investment by British fund managers.

There are many threats to the future of the asset management industry in Britain, including international competition as discussed below. But it is clear to the author

UK-managed equities by region, 2006-2011
Source: Investment Management Association, 2010-11 Survey

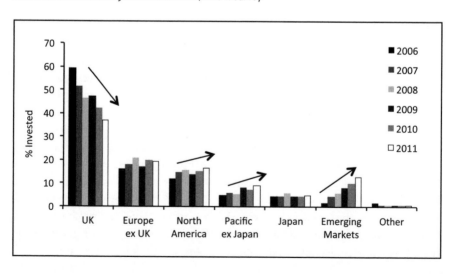

that the volume, complexity, cost and intrusiveness of regulation (well-meaning or not) is a serious threat, especially if it is not replicated to the same degree elsewhere.

Hedge funds – unjustified bogeyman?

Humans fear the vulture as the harbinger of death. Many people seem to see hedge funds as the powerful and secretive vultures of global finance, and they are readily portrayed as one of the key causes of the Global Financial Crisis (GFC). The truth is far from this and much more complex.

What are they? Hedge funds are actively managed private investment funds that invest across a very wide range of markets and strategies. Each strategy has its own risk-return characteristics. The four main types of strategy are macro (anticipating macroeconomic trends); event-driven (looking for valuation inconsistencies in corporate transactional events); directional (generally stock picking based on market movements or trends and including long/short funds); relative value (taking advantage of relative discrepancies in price between securities and non-directional or market-neutral). There are also multi-strategy funds, fund of hedge funds and managed futures funds which do not fit neatly in to the above.

The interests of the investment manager, who is kept legally separate from the fund itself, are aligned with performance. Most managers, who typically invest money of their own in the funds they manage, aim to achieve a positive return for their investors whatever the market. Fees are generally divided into a management fee based on the level of assets under management, and initially designed to cover costs, and a performance fee, which is often charged over a fixed or floating "hurdle rate" like a global equity index or interest rate or just a fixed percentage. Whilst earnings at the top of the industry are far higher than any other, and attract the headlines, many hedge funds are small and failure can mean not getting paid. Most funds are open-ended and investors can withdraw their money. This can lead to the fund closing down.

Early hedge fund investors were often wealthy individuals but they have become increasingly popular with institutional investors (eg pension and insurance companies) and they constitute about two-thirds of investors currently. A key attraction is the additional diversification of portfolio risk a hedge fund investment represents. According to The Wall Street Journal total assets under management was about $2.1 trillion in April 2012. BarclayHedge estimate this figure to be $2.35 trillion in the first quarter of 2013, including $485 billion of assets held by fund of funds. Whilst hedge funds posted disappointing returns in 2008, the losses were far less than the actual debt or equity markets movements and much better than "long-only" mutual fund performance. Since then, returns have been less consistent than in the period before the GFC.

Are hedge funds a threat to the world's financial system? Not according to Ben Bernanke, the Chairman of the Federal Reserve Board, the US central bank. In testimony to the US House of Representatives Financial Services Committee in 2009 he said he "would not think that any hedge fund or private equity fund would become a systemically-critical firm individually"[1]. The UK Financial Services Authority, which began its Hedge Fund Survey in 2009, reported in August 2012: "results from the March 2012 HFS suggest that risks to financial stability through the 'market' channel are limited at the time of the latest survey"[2]. Whilst organisations such as the National Bureau of Economic Research and the European Central Bank have cited hedge funds as posing a systemic risk (ie instability across the financial system), the fact is that most funds are small and not highly leveraged, especially when compared to investment banks. Hedge funds fail all the time (and there have been some spectacular failures like LTCM in 1998 and Bernard Madoff's fund in 2008) but the author's understanding is that no financial assistance has been provided to hedge funds by the British (or US) taxpayer - in marked contrast to the treatment of some commercial and investment banks.

Do they pay enough tax? This is a difficult question to answer. Many funds are established in offshore financial centres to avoid adverse tax consequences for their foreign and tax-exempt investors, such as pension funds or endowments. Most investment managers are themselves located onshore in major financial centres like New York, London, Hong Kong or Singapore. About three-quarters of European hedge funds are located in Britain. HM Revenue & Customs have recently proposed to clamp down on (legal) tax avoidance by UK-based hedge funds, private equity firms and other investment management partnerships. A key issue here is the funneling of performance fees through corporate rather than individual board members at lower tax rates.

---

[1]   "Testimony of Douglas Lowenstein President/CEO Private Equity Council House Financial Services Committee", House gov. 6 October 2009. Sourced from Wikipedia.

[2]   Financial Services Authority, "Assessing the possible sources of systemic risk from hedge funds", August 2012.

Are they transparent? Unlike mutual funds or unit trusts, hedge funds are private entities and are not obliged to disclose their detailed financial activities to the outside world. Investors in hedge funds understandably have much better access. The implicit assumption is that the investors have to do their own homework on the funds and there are many consultancies that offer these "due diligence" style services to asset allocators.

However, as part of the huge wave of regulation that has descended on top of the global financial services industry, the Alternative Investment Fund Managers Directive (AIFMD) was passed by the European Parliament and Council of the European Union in June 2011 and came into force in July 2013. It has a sweeping remit, including hedge and private equity fund managers wherever they are based that manage or market alternative investment funds established in the European Union. The European Securities and Markets Authority has also issued guidelines to national authorities including on key AIFMD concepts and remuneration.

The Directive's supporters say that alternative investment managers are too lightly regulated and are not subject to the same level of regulation as their mutual and pension fund cousins who are subject to UCITS (Undertakings for Collective Investment in Transferable Securities) regulation. Detractors point to the rising costs of compliance and many fund management groups are complaining about the sheer weight of regulation.

The Asian threat to the City is real

The British financial services industry has a sizeable market share compared to its proportion of global domestic product (GDP). Finance made up 9.6% of British GDP in 2011. This was two-thirds more than the 5.7% EU country average. As we have seen, the asset management industry represents a key part of this.

Whilst London will retain its advantages of language (English is the lingua franca of global commerce), and time zone (bridging the Americas-Asia gap), Britain risks waking up in ten years time to find that London is no longer a top three global financial centre. Paris and Frankfurt seem less of a threat perhaps than Singapore, Hong Kong, Dubai, New York or even Shanghai further into the future as China opens up its capital account. The name of the game for ambitious finance centres is "clustering". A key element in London's historic success has been its ability to bring together in a relatively small geographic area a sufficiently broad and deep financial services talent pool. If you can replicate this, backed up by appropriate IT and

Singapore's financial district
Source: Bing images

physical infrastructure and a pleasant and tax-friendly place to live with good schools and other facilities, then you become quickly competitive.

The authorities responsible for London's competitor cities are doing their utmost to lure away banks, law firms, insurance companies, shipping companies, commodity brokers, headhunters and independent finance companies of all types. You only have to see the new finance district skylines of Hong Kong, Shanghai, Singapore and Dubai to witness the scale of the ambition.

Financial services generate about 11% of Singapore's GDP and employ 5% of its workforce. The equivalent figures for Hong Kong are 15% and 6%. English and Chinese are spoken in both cities and both are strong in contract law given their historical links to Britain. Whilst Hong Kong is China's financial gateway (and worries about Shanghai's rise), Singapore is viewed as being more politically neutral than Hong Kong and attracts Indian, Indonesian, Japanese and Korean investors. Crucially, both are seen as finance-friendly. A 2011 survey that asked finance service executives where they would most like to work ranked Singapore as number one, New York two and London three. London's ranking was down three percentage points at only 22%. The table on the page opposite refers to a separate survey by PwC, the consultancy, and appeared in a 24 July article in The Financial Times entitled "Singapore loosens Swiss grip on wealth management". Note London's position slipping from second to fourth.

The Investment Management Association 2010-11 annual report noted the strong growth in assets under management in Hong Kong and Singapore, and said that if

Europe is losing out to Asia in wealth management
Source: FT; PwC survey result of 275 industry professionals

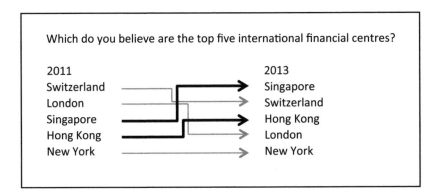

current growth rates were maintained, Hong Kong and Singapore would have combined assets under management of £4 trillion by 2020 (although this would represent just over a third of the projected assets of the UK). The same report also quotes from one of the interviews the survey conducted (one of thirty senior executives at 20 IMA member firms):

> "It would not surprise me if, ten years down the line, our organization had moved its headquarters to Asia. Asia is easily up there with the most important regions for us; not just in terms of revenue or assets, but also if you think about where the economic growth is, and where the savings are going to be over the next 40-50 years".

Another key issue to remember with fund management is that it is "asset light". The main business cost - and risk - is people who leave at night and hopefully all return the following morning. If the conditions of employment change sufficiently or the opportunity cost of staying put rises enough, then talent will move. Retaining that talent is crucial for companies, as well as financial centres. Whilst large-scale asset management companies clearly have a substantial real estate footprint and invest large amounts of cash flow in information technology, the majority of smaller firms are nimble in terms of their ability to transfer personnel or even legal incorporation (although the obstacles to this are growing as regulation tightens globally). Anecdotal evidence suggests that the likes of Singapore and Hong Kong, as well as other locations in countries like Switzerland and Ireland, continue to attract fund management executives away from Britain. Larger firms can re-locate within themselves.

High-powered civil servants running city states like Singapore understand this, which is why asset managers with assets of less than S$250 million and 30 qualified investors are subject to lighter regulations than those above these thresholds.

There is also a broader point here. Britain's obsession with "Europe" comes with a high economic price tag, not just in terms of EU over-regulation and unproductive employment laws, but in the opportunity cost of not being fully engaged in the highest growth areas of the world. The world's economic centre is shifting East (and slightly South) and has been for years. In 1980 it was located at a point in the middle of the Atlantic Ocean reflecting the dominance of the US economy, but by 2008 it had drifted east of Bucharest, the capital of Romania as emerging economies grew. Emerging countries' real GDP now constitutes 30% of global real GDP, a share as large as that of the USA. Extrapolation projects the centre of gravity to lie between India and China by 2050. The graphic below shows, in 3 year intervals, the WECG 1980-2007 in black and projections for 2010 – 2049 in dark grey.

The world's economic centre of gravity – going East, 1980-2049
Source: Danny Quah, Economics Department, London School of Economics and Political Science and LSE Global Governance as at January 2011

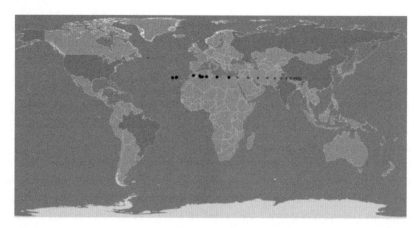

According to The Economist, emerging economies like China, India, Indonesia, Brazil and Turkey accounted for three-quarters of global GDP growth between 2000 and 2010. In 2013 emerging countries will produce the majority of the world's goods and services for the first time since the Industrial Revolution, whilst the world's next billion consumers are almost all going to live outside Europe. Consumer spending in emerging countries already accounts for 15% of world GDP in real terms. Europe, and in particular the Eurozone, in contrast is likely to continue to decline on a relative basis in part driven by its demographics, but also structural issues like low expenditure on R&D and a relative absence of EU universities in global rankings.

Share of World GDP growth* (%)
Source: IMF (2011)   *measured in purchasing power parity

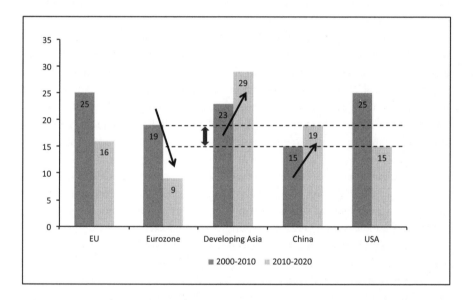

The author was struck by the following paragraph in "The Europe 2020 Strategy" report of 2010 by the Centre for European Policy Studies in Brussels (note the location of this organisation):

> "Given that the emerging economies, chiefly China, are set to outgrow the EU over the next decade by a large margin, it is clear that success for the Europe 2020 agenda will be measured not by whether the EU is able to maintain a top position in economic league tables, but rather whether it can manage relative decline in such a way that the standard of living of the greying EU population still increases modestly."

Most people's reaction to this, and certainly the author's, is "great, so that's what we have to look forward to" – a stunning lack of ambition reminiscent of Britain's "managed decline" of the 1970's. How about raising productivity?

Britain needs to turn away from the burden of further EU regulation and legislation. She needs to offset a growing trade imbalance with the EU (and particularly Germany) via more trade with friendly Commonwealth nations such as Singapore, Malaysia, Australia, Canada, South Africa and India. Indeed, trade with these nations is on an upward trend. Of course, Britain must also trade more with major economies like China, Brazil and Russia. Amazingly, the author understands that just 4% of British exports go to the BRIC countries – it feels like the political class has been asleep for the past twenty years.

Whilst China's growth rate is likely to decelerate, its economy would still double in just 14 years in real terms if it averaged only 5% annual growth. The good news is that as countries like China morph from focusing on investment-driven production to a more high value-add consumer-led expansion, Britain is well positioned to sell more goods and services in industries of the future. What are these? They are financial services, media, design, advertising, fashion, technology and high end manufacturing – industries where Britain has somewhat of a competitive advantage.

As emerging countries continue to grow, their huge savings offer an enormous opportunity for British asset management firms prepared to venture overseas. In fact the efficient investment of this huge pool of money is important for the stability of the global financial system as excess emerging markets savings rates, and the glut of capital this represented, were a key driver of highly imprudent credit provision in the run up to the crisis of 2008 and subsequent global recession.

China saved 54.3% of its GDP in 2012 according to the IMF, the world's highest ratio. Total Chinese savings are now about Rmb 20 trillion, or £2.1 trillion. This equates to about £1,600 per capita. The ASEAN countries of south-east Asia also offer huge potential for UK fund management. Although the risks are higher in terms of governance and policy, the growth rates are attractive. Fund management houses that have or do find the right local partner should do very well as Asia gradually internationalises its massive savings pools.

Anthony Wilkinson

With 24 years experience across the fields of corporate finance, stock-broking and investment management, Anthony Wilkinson is now responsible for advising and managing US$1 billion of investors' savings as Chief Investment Officer of the Sustainable Equity group inside Deutsche Bank's Asset and Wealth Management arm. In 2006 Anthony co-founded Asia's first clean technology public equities fund, which grew to encompass private equity clean tech fund management. He has lived in Asia for much of the past seventeen years. Anthony read Joint Honours French and Politics at the University of Bristol having completed a Short Service Limited Commission in the British Army. Until recently he was Chairman of Conservatives Abroad Singapore where he successfully campaigned for improved voting rights and procedures for Britain's millions of expats. With the support of The Freedom Association, Anthony organised and spoke at a fringe meeting at the 2012 Conservative Party conference entitled "Kill the City, kill Britain".
Anthony writes in a personal capacity.

Chapter 6

An engine room, not a casino: the City's role through history

Abhishek Majumdar

Introduction

It is difficult, when contemplating the modern world, not to surrender to the human prejudice that strongly prefers the tangible to the ephemeral. Like all prejudices, this one is rooted in collective experience: the memory of our days as pack animals forces a focus on that which is in front of us, that which we can see, grip or smell.

But as our civilisation has developed, we have learned to place value on the intangible: on promises, commitments, favours and debts. Through money and financial instruments such as bonds and shares, we have quantified these human ties and made them freely transferable, enabling the spread of prosperity and the creation of wealth.

The aim of this chapter is to outline the activities that take place in the City, describe briefly their benefits to Britain and the world, and provide some historical context for them. Too often, these intangible activities, which can appear extraneous, are dismissed as being useless except in that they make money for their executors. To many, the City is parasitical, extracting value from the 'real' economy of manufactured goods and products. This is a dangerous fallacy and those that subscribe to it have misunderstood the role of financial services in an advanced economy.

Simply put, a free market requires money and investment to flow quickly to where it is needed most, and this, in reduced terms, is the City's role. Without this function, stagnation and inefficiency abound, with capital hoarded for unproductive uses, like medieval keeps full of gold.

Of course, antipathy towards the unknown is natural, and the City performs such a head-achingly wide array of specialised functions that each is almost inexplicable to the casual onlooker. But little that goes on in the Square Mile is rocket science. There are three broad functions that I think summarise roughly the majority of financial activity in the City. These are: to transfer risk to those who have the appetite for it from those that do not; to provide a pool from which productive enterprises can draw capital; and to create a liquid market in which securities can be traded. The happy by-product of these activities is substantial tax revenue for the British exchequer and employment for thousands, but these are secondary benefits which are adequately enumerated elsewhere.

The chart below shows clearly the importance of intangible products to Britain: financial services and insurance are two of our largest net exports. These are wealth generating exports every bit as real and beneficial as coal or cotton or cars.

Net UK exports, 2012 Source: ONS

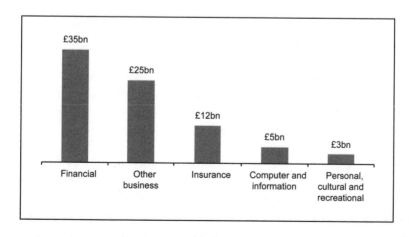

A nation's power and influence is founded not on its military but its prosperity. History is littered with the corpses of empires built on the sands of militarism. Apart from the immorality of violent conquest, an economy based on loot will subsist only temporarily, as long as the oppressor maintains its strength and the loot does not run out. Britain's past is not without its regrettable episodes, but its prosperity today is based firmly on trade, which forms part of a long and proud British mercantile tradition. As the hub in the wheel of the economy, the City is part of the foundation of our country's present and future greatness.

The City as a risk exchange

Free market capitalism rewards risk taking. Hard work and merit are important, but no rational economic system can depend on them alone. Rather, there must be commensurate rewards on offer to those with the courage to take on the risk of embarking on new ventures otherwise these would never take place.

However, the management of risk is also essential. If the consequences of failure are total, a new venture must have profound riches as its reward in order to be worthwhile. For many in the Renaissance era, the fabled wealth of the New World represented just such a reward, and the voyages in search of treasure and trade were the result.

The expense of fitting out and undertaking these voyages limited them to those of substantial means. The ability to absorb large losses was also important. When this was the case, Britain was dependent on the whims of rich men for setting up trading posts, and while she was fortunate to have a large stock of men with suitably large appetites for such undertakings, it was not until the advent of insurance that this process began to accelerate.

Seen from this perspective, it is clear that the development of the insurance industry, which has some claim to be the foundation stone of the modern City, was crucial to the rise of Britain as an early superpower. Without this, the maritime endeavours that led to the creation of Empire would never have taken place, and Britain would never have found foreign markets for the goods and exports produced during the Industrial Revolution.

By pooling the potential losses from all ventures, the risk of failure, while disastrous to a single merchant, was shared among many. In the absence of any state direction or coercion, a natural order emerged, governed by the private profit motive, represented in this case by the insurance premium that replaced a potential huge loss with a real, small one. Via this simple mechanism the world of overseas trade was made accessible for a wide class of merchants.

The City's insurance industry has historically been dominated by Lloyd's of London, which began as a series of discussions in Edward Lloyd's coffee shop in Tower Street in the late 17th century. At the time that these gatherings began in earnest, the Glorious Revolution had just taken place and Anglo-Dutch animosity had been transformed into an alliance - an alliance which led directly to the usurpation of the Dutch Republic by Britain as the world's dominant maritime power, and the eventual replacement of Amsterdam as the world's principal trading hub by London. Just as now, the gathering of businessmen was predicated on commonality of interest and fed by the steady flow of information, in this case shipping news, and lubricated by coffee (in those days harder stuff than today's frothy drinks). And just as now, no city in the world had a God-given right to dominance, as the swift eclipse of Amsterdam showed.

In time the concept of insurance has expanded throughout the economy. The premium paid by an individual or business represents a simple swap of uncertainty for certainty, with the latter priced at a small percentage of overall spending or profit, according to the scale of the uncertainty being removed. This powerful trade spurs economic activity by allowing the buyer of insurance to focus on other, more profitable or enjoyable activities than worrying about future losses. While shipping was the spur, insurance has become available for, inter alia, property, life and infrastructure, as well as insurance firms themselves (reinsurance).

The City, as a pioneer in this industry, has built a substantial body of expertise which it is now seeking to deploy abroad and in ever more parts of the economy. As global populations age and healthcare becomes more expensive, insurance provides part of the solution to achieving widespread and high quality care, easing the burden on taxpayers and sharing it with the growing economic middle class around the world, who can now for the first time afford to pay regular premiums. As the home of Europe's largest, and the world's third largest insurance industry, Britain is uniquely placed to exploit this future growth.

One measure of prosperity is the penetration of insurance into a nation's economy, and on this measure there are still millions of people who are one fire, one flood or one illness away from desperate poverty, traditional family structures and charity notwithstanding. Welfare is one answer, and if controlled is a proper constituent of a civilized country. But state action requires a financially healthy state, in the absence of which the outcome is devastation, as we have seen with floods in Pakistan and earthquakes in Haiti. Insurance is the free market's answer to managing risk, and its global spread should be encouraged, with City firms leading the way. This is a future export that Britain should enthusiastically embrace.

The City as a capital pool

Poverty comes in many forms; a lack of ready funds is only the most obvious. A more insidious form of poverty can be seen in the world's poorer societies, which serves to keep entire countries trapped in subsistence activity, unable to achieve the 'escape velocity' needed for their economies to grow and create wealth. This is lack of capital: the poverty of low investment. It presses an endless cycle of unproductive work upon its victims, which at the best of times meets the immediate needs of the worker and at the worst, leaves him without food and medicine. Without the ability to safely store and invest surpluses, each year resembles the last and no progress is made.

Capital is the means by which the surplus derived from productive daily activity is re-invested into the economy. It is present wherever humans have traded freely and been able to keep their profit without worry of seizure, and represents an investment in the future. The aphorism about teaching a man to fish so that he never goes hungry, as opposed to giving him fish so he doesn't go hungry this evening, is a neat summary of this fact. The fishing rod and the skill to use it represent capital, while the fish is consumption.

In a primitive economy, feudal structures ensure that capital is hoarded. Instead of being put to productive use, wealth is kept under guard as a rational protection against violence, upheaval and famine. For Britain, a happy combination of Enlightenment liberalism, technological progress in agriculture and industry, and naval prowess removed this need and created the environment needed for investment in the machinery and infrastructure of the industrial era. Until this point, the resources that would transform Britain lay buried. To reach them required demand, and capital.

Capital accumulation is often frowned upon and derided as unsophisticated, or even blamed for stagnation. In fact, it is the basis of civilization. While consumption can only drive present profits, investment builds the future. The lesson of the dynamic Victorian era should be that savings and investments are just as important as consumption, and that demand-led growth is no substitute for real, productive growth.

Between the union of England and Scotland in 1707 and the death of Queen Victoria in 1901, annual coal production grew by over 9,000 per cent. During roughly the same era, there was a corresponding and not coincidental over ten-fold increase in gross domestic fixed capital. The small investors of the new middle class, from prosperous farmers to merchants to modest landowners, were investing their money for the first time on a mass scale. As this network of trading grew, the City naturally developed its importance as a financial centre, particularly as the amounts needed to finance, for example, railways and canals, grew in size.

In 1698, a group of stock dealers were expelled from the Royal Exchange for rowdiness. Like the Oxonian scholars that founded Cambridge, they took their revenge by establishing themselves elsewhere and prospering. With other like-minded men, they took up residence in a coffee house in Change Alley, sowing the seeds for what would become the London Stock Exchange. Like Lloyd's of London, the purpose of these meetings was to trade risk. Unlike at Lloyd's, the risk was not to be pooled and minimised; instead it was to be sold to whomever wanted it and was willing to pay for it. Investors could buy shares in companies, allowing those companies to invest the new money and allowing investors to share in success.

This system of raising equity capital proved profoundly successful, and assisted the growth of numerous British giants, from Rolls Royce to ICI. While the market fell into stagnation during the 1970s, the 'Big Bang' package of deregulation passed by the Thatcher government spurred the markets and ensured international competitiveness.

In 2012 the LSE oversaw the raising of c. £10bn of equity finance. The alternative investments market (AIM), launched in 1995, has provided a route for smaller companies to raise equity finance, crucial in bridging the gap between early-stage venture capital investment and large-scale capital raising for more mature concerns. Since then, several billions of pounds of equity has been raised for UK listed companies (see chart over), money that has, among other uses, funded capital expenditure that in turn drives growth.

London has, of course, numerous natural advantages in a global economy - its positioning between sunrise in New York and sunset in Tokyo has been a not insubstantial factor in its success. But one of its major victories came in the form of an own goal by the opposition when, in 2002, George W Bush signed the Sarbanes-Oxley act into US law. Sarbox, as it became known, was an understandable reaction to the wave of outrageous corporate crimes uncovered in the late 1990s and early 2000s, of which the most widely known was that involving Enron. This public scandal, which involved the use of an approach to hiding debt off balance sheet enthusiastically adopted by New Labour, led Bush to sign an aggressive piece of legislation forcing several onerous requirements onto listed companies.

Money raised on AIM
Source: London Stock Exchange

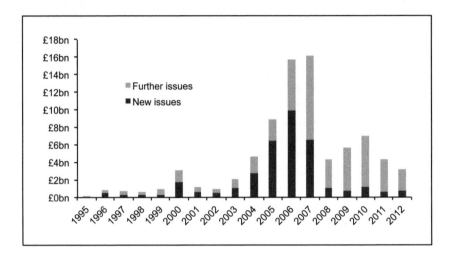

As a result, international firms seeking a listing destination increasingly chose London over New York, with the LSE gaining an advantage over both the NYSE and Nasdaq. The relatively light regulatory environment in the UK has not been without its critics. In recent months, governance scandals have highlighted the need for care when welcoming international firms to the London markets. Nevertheless, the experience of Sarbox demonstrates the ability of governments to squander economic advantages.

While individual investors are important to the success of the equity markets, the UK is also home to numerous asset management firms, which between them (according to the Investment Management Association) manage £4.2 trillion of client money, £2.6 trillion of this being British funds. Much of this is pension money that flows through the City, finding a home in shares and bonds. As society ages and pension schemes move towards a defined contribution structure, the role of the City will become more vital still. With pensioners relying on personal or corporate pensions instead of governments, it is essential that those schemes earn adequate returns, which means they must be invested well. Tackling the on-going global challenge of low returns, created in part by the inflationary activities of central banks, will be one of the City's most critical jobs in the coming decades.

Capital does not, of course, just come in the form of equity and shares. The debt markets are the other pillar for companies and (in particular) governments and municipalities seeking capital. Since the late 18th century, when Barings first arranged loans for the British government, and later for the King of Portugal among other foreign clients, the City has been an active marketplace for bonds, loans and other debt instruments. In 2008, according to the Bank for International Settlements, the UK was the world leader in issuance of international bonds, with 30 per cent of the global total. The UK bond market itself is expected to grow, as Western Europe in general moves gradually to a more US-style debt market, in which companies use bonds as well as banks to borrow money for growth and investment. This long-term trend is one the City is well-placed to exploit.

In other ways, London's future as a capital pool can be seen already, developing on the fringes of the City near Old Street. Here, new ventures, mostly in the technology sector, are establishing offices and drawing investment from angel investors and venture capital firms. As these succeed, their founders become rich and are driven to re-invest in other ventures, creating the kind of start-up ecosystem that made Silicon Valley the home of several billion-dollar companies. Just as in centuries past, companies that are making the world a better place through their products and services are using London as a base, putting capital to work.

The City as a liquidity provider

One of the triumphs of the human race has been to make commitments transferable; in other words to invent money. As a unit of exchange, money allows value to be made liquid.

Liquidity allows business owners to realise their investments by selling their stakes or borrowing against them, and in so doing creates clear incentives for holders of capital to invest. Without liquidity, an entrepreneur would face the option of shutting down a profitable concern or retiring and handing it to somebody else for free, or otherwise be compelled to run the business in perpetuity to reap value. Furthermore, if at any point he wanted to attract new capital - assuming he was able to procure any - he would need to do so at a deeply discounted valuation, given that the new investor would never be able to get rid of his or her new investment.

While the equity and bond markets are, as discussed previously, a vital source of new (primary) money for businesses, they are also an essential secondary market, which is to say that they are a forum in which investors can buy from or sell to other investors. There are myriad such markets in the City, many of them outside formal venues like the LSE and known as OTC (over-the-counter) markets, involving trading in almost all asset classes.

The secondary markets allow for the proper pricing of risk. A share of a company in its early days is a very different proposition to a share of a large, mature company, and therefore being able to buy and sell those shares is critical to allowing investors to place their capital where they feel most comfortable doing so. Similarly a bond can begin as a safe investment but become riskier when the company or government that issued it runs into difficulties. To remove liquidity would therefore be to force the same risk-reward profile onto all investors, driving many out of the market and starving companies of capital. The range of securities traded in the City allows investors to develop bespoke portfolios to manage their risk exposure, with a judicious mixture of high, medium and low-risk investments creating a balance.

Loans can be, and are, traded on the secondary market, allowing for flexibility under financial distress. When loans are originally made, they are mostly done so on the basis of stable cash flows and predictable risks. If a company then starts to trade poorly, the migration of its debt into the hands of investors with ever larger risk appetites allows it to find a middle ground between full recovery and outright bankruptcy. Restructuring arrangements can lead to the new debt holders converting the money owed them into equity, thereby reducing the ailing company's debt burden, wiping out its shareholders - a proper consequence of excessive risk taken by equity holders - and implement a turnaround strategy. This is one example of a 'win-win' situation permitted by a healthy secondary market.

Trading is a poorly understood activity, attracting as it does derogatory labels such as 'casino' banking. Part of its economic function lies in its acceleration of the process of price discovery. To use a simple analogy, apples sold in Covent Garden for £1 each and Camden for 50 pence would bestow super-profits on the Covent Garden sellers, while the Camden sellers would be discouraged from selling apples at all. A trader would acquire the cheaper fruit and, assuming minimal cost of transport, sell it more expensively. In time, other traders will notice the money to be made from buying low and selling high, and pile in themselves. As demand in Camden spikes, so does supply in Covent Garden, and prices approach 'equilibrium'. The example is crude but it illustrates the principle: traders can profit by exploiting inefficiency and in so doing, remove it. Information is spread more quickly than in the absence of such profiteering and the process of pricing is accelerated.

Not all trading, of course, is of this variety (known as arbitrage). Much is, once again, a question of risk. A tyre manufacturing company that earns its revenue in the US in dollars and cents but pays its workers and suppliers in Euros does not want to face losses should the Euro strengthen against the dollar - nor incidentally is it much interested in making profits when the exchange rate moves in the other direction it is favour. Its job is to manufacture tyres, and nothing else. In the City, traders can, at the company's request, remove this uncertainty by selling it a hedge whereby, for example, it can swap dollars for Euros at some fixed future exchange rate. When this happens, the risk and associated reward of currency swings has effectively left the tyre company and gone to reside elsewhere. The proper home for this risk is with someone who is willing to take it on because they think they can make money from the currency swing.

In other words, to state the mechanism in simple terms, the tyre company has absolved itself of the need to bet on whether the dollar will rise against the Euro or vice-versa. The trader that thinks the dollar will rise has taken on this bet, and must find herself a counterparty who is willing to bet against. This has the appearance of gambling but is nothing but. It is, rather, controlled risk taking by those whose job it is to take risks. As we have seen with insurance, the City has transferred risk from those who do not want it to those who do.

As can be seen below, the UK is the world's leading centre of foreign exchange activity. This lead position dates partly from the 1960s, when the financier Siegmund Warburg established the first 'eurobond' (a bond with a coupon payable in dollars but issued outside the US), pioneering what would become a trillion dollar industry.

% of global Forex turnover, 2010
Source: Bank for International Settlements

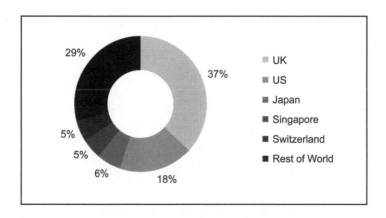

It can also be traced to the 1970s, when a combination of timely deregulation and the collapse of the Bretton Woods system led to a floating market in currencies, which London came to dominate.

The principle of price discovery extends to commodities also. The London Metals Exchange conducts the majority of the world's trading in non-ferrous metals, and serves to establish pricing for products from copper to cobalt. While these trading activities are often dismissed as 'speculation', they are a crucial part of the global economy. Miners look to prices when making critical investment decisions that govern the spending of money on large projects, and without a liquid market pricing signals can become distorted. Derivative instruments that track the energy markets, such as oil futures, also allow the activity of physical drilling to be conducted efficiently and precisely, with money invested where and when it is most needed, thanks to the rapid flow of pricing information allowed by the markets.

Another vital part of the secondary markets is the arena of corporate deal-making, sometimes referred to as M&A (mergers and acquisitions). Here, shareholders and company management teams are sold advice on the buying and selling of companies themselves, which is a more complex and slower-moving process than trading in liquid securities. Deals such as these can be transformational for companies in finding synergies or enhancing growth, and have encouraged the growth of a (relatively) new asset class: private equity, which involves the ownership of entire companies rather than shares. A healthy M&A market is important for the sweeping changes it is able to effect; often a firm needs new management or wholesale restructuring before its true potential can be realised.

The number of firms providing M&A advice clustered in the City illustrates the power of collective expertise. A business that can in theory be conducted largely over the telephone and via email, requiring not a great deal of technology, still takes place overwhelmingly in the Square Mile as opposed to elsewhere in the country, thanks to the clustering of professionals there.

The secondary markets, in summary, are not a 'casino', as they have on occasion been labelled. They are the lubricant of the economy, allowing the preferences of an individual with small amounts of money, moderate risk appetite and a desire for short-term profits to be calibrated with the preferences of a corporation for large-scale, high risk capital investment over a long time period, or allowing commodities to find a price at which buyers are comfortable buying and sellers selling. Without this liquidity and without efficient pricing, the economy would be stagnant, with all the quiet devastation that entails.

Pooling talent and raising taxes

A fifth of UK graduates in employment find work in London, with many gravitating to the City. While this appears to bestow unhealthy power on the City, it hides two important facts. One is that a city which is attractive to skilled employees globally will attract local skilled employees too; in other words it is to be expected that Chinese engineers as well as international ones will want to go to Shanghai to find work. This kind of gravitational pull cannot be focused; it exerts its force everywhere - in other words, if we want talented foreigners to come and work in the City, we should expect that talented Britons will want to go and work there too. The alternatives are either that those skilled graduates go abroad, in which case the whole of Britain loses out, or that Manchester or Edinburgh or Bristol compete with London by becoming attractive global investment destinations themselves - an outcome all Britons should hope for.

The second important fact to consider is that the value created in London does not all accrue to London. City firms act for international clients on a large scale. They also act for British companies, helping them raise capital, achieve efficiency and expand. In this way, a graduate sitting in an office in EC1 can help a Yorkshire manufacturing company attract new investment and so develop its plant and create jobs in Yorkshire, without actually working there. Of course, firms in the City pursue profits and so will assist companies seeking to employ or manufacture in locations from Buenos Aires to Bamako, as opposed to focusing wholly or even mainly on helping British enterprises. But this again is a reflection of the City's strength, and the alternative is that such activities are conducted abroad instead of in London.

Finally we cannot ignore the role of the City as a tax generator and employer. These, in my opinion, are merely corollaries - they are secondary benefits. Nevertheless they are important considerations. If any other British industry generated as much for the Exchequer or employed as many people, it would be the recipient of more praise than criticism. On these terms, the City deserves the same.

Conclusion

The image of Britons as a prim, orderly and conservative people is a relatively new one. While not an undesirable image, it is inaccurate when considered in a wider historic context.

When Napoleon foolishly derided England as a nation of shopkeepers, he was only half right: for many decades smuggling, as well shopkeeping, enjoyed great popularity, with the coastline perforated with sheltered rendezvous into which tea and gin, among other contraband, flowed in huge quantities. This was only part of a maritime adventuring tradition centuries old.

During the 19th century, British inventors, engineers and entrepreneurs led an explosion of innovation in the name of both science and private profit, pushing ever more radical ideas and new technology that would become part of everyday life.

Trade and entrepreneurship in their rawest forms are therefore old British traditions. Capitalism is not some foreign import but rather part of London's ancient fabric, and the City is at the core of this heritage.

This chapter has only skimmed the surface of the City's modern complexity and dynamism, but what should clearly emerge is a picture of an historic British asset playing a critical role in the global economy, driving the peaceful, scientific and capitalistic progress of the 21st century.

Abhishek Majumdar

Abhishek works in the City as a corporate finance professional, and has advised clients on a range of transactions including acquisitions, disposals, flotations and restructurings. He is a Conservative party member and stood for election to Westminster City Council in 2010. Abhishek read Physics at Oxford University.